DEALER GUIDES

ENGLISH
SILVER
HALL-MARKS

Including the Marks of Origin on
SCOTTISH & IRISH SILVER PLATE
GOLD, PLATINUM & SHEFFIELD PLATE

With 300 of the more important
MAKERS MARKS FROM 1697–1900

edited by

Judith Banister

with lists of
English, Scottish and Irish
Hall-marks and Makers' Marks
from Circa 1554

LONDON
W. FOULSHAM & Co. Ltd.
NEW YORK   TORONTO   CAPE TOWN   SYDNEY

W. FOULSHAM & CO. LTD.,

Bennetts Close, Cippenham, Berks, England

ISBN 0-572-02999-3

© Copyright Design and Layout 1970
New Edition 2004
BELASCO

Printed in Great Britain by
St Edmundsbury Press Ltd.,
Bury St Edmunds, Suffolk

CONTENTS

ACKNOWLEDGEMENTS

The Publishers extend their thanks to the Masters of the Assay Offices of Dublin, Sheffield and Birmingham for the advice, guidance and material for reproduction which they were kind enough to supply.

In particular sincere thanks are extended to the Goldsmiths Company for the continuance support and assistance which they gave and for the right to reproduce the majority of Makers' marks from their records.

Also Acknowledged is the material reprinted from Goldsmiths & Their Marks by Sir Charles Jackson, Dover Publications, New York through whom permissions were obtained.

Other Dealer Guides

English Pottery and Porcelain Hallmarks
English Pewter Touchmarks
Victorian Painters' Monograms

PREFACE

The intention underlying the publication of this Pocket Identification Guide has been to provide, for Collectors and Dealers alike, a portable reference source to the Assay Office Marks *and* more important Makers' Marks found on British silver and gold. The marks on platinum, as well as those on the most commonly encountered Sheffield plate, are also included.

In the tables containing the Assay Office Marks, it will be seen that each cycle has been contained in one box and that to the outside edge of each box an additional panel has been added. This layout was chosen to allow for the inclusion in the panels of an enlarged Assay Office Symbol, Date Letter and gold quality marks which we hope will provide for quicker visual location when "flipping through" the pages. This will be of value not only to those who do know something of hall-marking but also to those new collectors who know nothing of the devices adopted by the various Assay Offices. It is assumed that these Collectors will carefully read the Introduction but for them we would explain that having located the *style* of town mark and date letter in the outside panel all of the remaining marks on the piece in question must be checked against those reproduced in the box. This should confirm that the right period has been located and provide a date of Assay against the relevant date letter.

During the earliest working periods of some of the Assay Offices there is little consistency in the design of marks applied to silver. They change so frequently in the cycle boxes that it has been impossible to include anything very worthwhile in the exterior panels. For consistency, however, we have included the design that seems to be most representative of those in the boxes and hope that they will be of some value.

Finally, attention is drawn to the details of monarchs in each panel. These are included to show which of the sovereigns were reigning during each cycle. Where only one name is given, it can be taken that throughout that period there was no accession to the throne. Where there is a change of rule during the cycle, both monarchs and the date of accession are given.

The Makers' Marks found in the third section of the book are in the main of those whose work was done in London; though obviously we have included the most important makers from Birmingham, Dublin, Edinburgh and Sheffield. We have confined our coverage of them to the period 1697 to 1900 which we felt represented the period from which most antique silver is currently available. Obviously to include every silver maker of that period is out of the question in a book of this length and we therefore compiled a list of renowned or prolific silver makers and illustrated those of their marks which would ensure the identification of all of their work. Our reference source has been the Official records held by the Goldsmiths' Company in London whose permission and kind assistance we had in being allowed to photograph the marks entered by the London makers in the record books. For this reason we can reasonably claim that the section on Makers' Marks is one of the most accurate records available.

The only qualifying factor we would wish to place on the above statement is that though every mark represents an accurate impression of that entered in the record books, they are not necessarily proportionally accurate one to another. We have had to enlarge each mark for ease of identification but because of the great variety in their sizes and the standard width of our page, have been unable to achieve a standard degree of magnification.

Introduction
SILVER HALL-MARKS

Hall-marks are the authenticating marks struck on all modern and most old English, Scottish and Irish silver and gold. Since 1st January 1975 it has been necessary by law to include them on platinum also. They are official marks, applied only after testing that the standard, or quality, of the metal is right, but the term has also come to embrace the maker's mark. The hall-marking system in Britain has a long history, and it can claim to be the oldest form of consumer protection in the country.

In medieval England, regulation of the goldsmith's craft (the term goldsmith was formerly used without distinction for gold- and silver-smith) was in the hands of the London Goldsmiths' Company. Scotland has never been under their jurisdiction, though after the Act of Union, duties and other London-made laws were applied there. Dublin, likewise, has its own Company, to which Charles I granted a Charter in 1637; in Ireland there was no duty on silver until 1730, and the King's head duty mark there, did not appear until 1807.

The earliest statute concerning gold and silver is that of 1238 A.D., when the standards of fineness were laid down, but the true beginning of hall-marking dates from 1300 A.D., when it was decreed that no piece of silver "was to depart out of the hands of the workers" until it had been assayed (or tested) and marked with the leopard's head. The standard of silver was to be sterling, or 92·5 per cent. pure, which was the same standard as the coinage. At the same time, the "Guardians of the Craft" were instructed to go out among the workers to make sure that the law was enforced, and it was further enacted that "in all good towns of England where there are goldsmiths" the same should apply, and that one of their number should go to London "to seek their sure touch."

The Maker's Mark
In order to supervise the craft, it was obvious that some way had to be found to identify the maker of substandard wares, and so in 1363 it was commanded that each Master Goldsmith should have his own mark, which had to be registered. In the past, the maker's mark took a variety of forms. Sometimes it was merely a symbol, perhaps his shop sign, or a rebus or pun on his name. Later, initials, often associated with one or more

symbols or devices, became common. In 1696, with the introduction of the new higher Britannia Standard, all makers had to re-register their marks, and a completely new style was ordered – the use of the first two letters of the surname. In 1720, when the old sterling standard was restored, so were the old-style marks. Indeed, some makers were using marks of different styles at the same time, so in 1739 all were ordered to re-register with new marks, and from then on most marks took the form of initials of forename and surname, with only an occasional additional symbol such as a crown or a mullet.

The Date Letter

Towards the end of the 15th century, continued complaints about substandard wares resulted in a ruling that the "Keeper of the Touch" – in fact, the Assay Master – should be responsible for maintaining the standard. Probably that led to the date letter system, devised to ascertain the year of assay (and so to trace offending maker and assay-master as well) but by a happy chance also the silver collector's invaluable guide. The first full cycle of date letters in London started with A in 1478, and continued in 20-year cycles (omitting J, and from V to Z) without a break until 1696, when a new series commenced with the new Britannia standard. Since then, each new cycle, differentiated by changing styles of letter and/or shields, has been unbroken.

Until 1974, establishing the date of an item was complicated by the fact that the lengths of each cycle and the year of commencement varied from one assay office to another. Furthermore, each assay office changed its date letter at a different time of year – London in May, Birmingham and Sheffield in June, Edinburgh in October. It is therefore important to consult the tables with great care. In 1975 all the remaining operational assay offices (London, Birmingham, Sheffield and Edinburgh) adopted the same lettering cycle, using the same date letter and changing it on January 1st. The Dublin Assay Office also now changes its date letter on January 1st, but unlike the UK offices it commenced a new cycle, at A, in 1986.

The Leopard's Head

From early documents, it appears that the leopard's head, which was crowned until 1821, was the standard mark, but from 1544, when the lion passant gardant was added to the hall-marks, it became more accurately the authoritative mark

8

of the Goldsmiths' Company, and today it remains as the London town mark. As the Company's mark of authority, it was used by several of the provincial assay offices in addition to their own town mark. In York and Newcastle it was used until those offices were closed in 1857 and 1883 respectively. In Chester it was used until 1838, in Exter until 1777, and it also appeared on the few known pieces of Bristol silver made about 1720-1760. Neither Birmingham nor Sheffield, understandably, used it, and it was seldom struck elsewhere, though various forms of leopard's head, usually debased, were used in East Anglia, in Shrewsbury and even in Jamaica. In 1821, for some unspecified reason, it was deprived of its crown.

The Lion Passant

Sometimes called the sterling mark, the lion passant gardant made its first appearance in 1544, at a period when the coinage, normally of sterling silver, was much debased. It was perhaps struck by the Goldsmiths' Company as an indication that their hall-marked wares were sterling, even if the coinage were not. In 1720 its use was extended to all the existing provincial English assay offices, and it was also adopted at Sheffield and Birmingham when they opened in 1773. In Chester, York and Sheffield the lion passant has always been *gardant*, that is, looking over its shoulder, but elsewhere it changed to being merely *passant* (looking ahead) in London in 1821, in Exeter in 1837, in Newcastle in 1846 and in Birmingham in 1875.

The Britannia Standard

In 1696, so extensive had become the melting and clipping of coinage that the silversmiths were forbidden to use the sterling standard for their wares, but had to use a new higher standard, 95·8 per cent. pure, or another 8 dwts. of silver to the pound troy. New hall-marks were ordered, the "figure of a woman commonly called Britannia" and the lion's head erased (torn off at the neck) replacing the lion passant and the leopard's head crowned. As noted above, a new series of date letters began in March 1697, and makers had to register new marks.

Since the Britannia standard silver was more expensive, the silversmiths began to clamour for the restoration of sterling, though some actually lodged a counter-petition to retain the higher standard, because of advantages in its working (it being softer) and on account of the export trade with Europe. Their pleas were acknowledged by the permission to retain the higher standard alongside sterling when the old standard was restored on June 1, 1720.

The Duty Mark

The price of restoration of sterling in 1720 was a duty of 6d. an ounce on wrought plate. This resulted in the practice known as "duty-dodging" by which some silversmiths avoided paying duty by incorporating pieces of plate bearing hall-marks into a new piece. The duty was removed in 1758, only to be re-imposed, at the same rate, in 1784. Payment of duty was, as before, exacted at the time of assay, but from 1784 until its abolition in 1890, the duty paid was recorded by another hall-mark, the sovereign's head mark. At first, from December 1, 1784, until May 1786, the king's head was incuse, but after that it appeared in cameo. The profiles of George III, George IV and William IV face to the right, the head of Queen Victoria to the left. The duty mark was also struck in Edinburgh from 1784 onwards, in Glasgow from 1819, and in Dublin from 1807. Curiously, some assay offices did not change the punch on the death of the sovereign, and William IV's head sometimes appears on Victorian silver made in Chester, Edinburgh, Glasgow, Newcastle, Sheffield and York as late as 1840 or 1841.

The Duty Drawback Mark, an incuse figure of Britannia standing, is almost certainly the rarest of all hall-marks. It was used for only eight months, from 1st December 1784 until July 1785, on plate exported from England. Being struck after the piece was polished and finished, it was liable to damage it, and was therefore withdrawn, silversmiths simply claiming drawback of duty against shipping notes or invoices.

Outside London

Many of the ancient ordinances and other documents mention goldsmiths outside London, and from time to time various towns have been named as Assay Towns and as Mint Towns. A few survived into the 18th century, and even into the 19th century, as assay towns – Chester, Norwich, Newcastle, Exeter and York, and, apparently, Bristol. For the rest, the wear and tear of the years, changing taste and the consignment of silver to the melting-pot for one reason or another has made the history of the provincial silversmiths of Britain both difficult to unravel and wholly absorbing. Considerable research has brought credible attribution of dozens of different marks to minor centres, and certain identification of many others, such as Barnstaple, Hull, Kings Lynn, Leeds, Plymouth, Taunton, Truro and so on.

The enforcement of the higher Britannia Standard appears to have put an end to one or two of the last centres of silversmithing that survived into the late 17th century. Indeed, the Act of 1696 actually completely ignored even the major provincial centres, and it was not until 1700 that the position was rectified so far as Chester, York, Norwich and Exeter were concerned, and even then Newcastle, a thriving centre of silversmithing right through the 18th century, was ignored until 1701.

Until 1700, only York and, to a lesser degree, Norwich, had any system of date letters, and by then both these towns were almost dormant. Exeter, Newcastle and Chester all continued to be active throughout the 18th century, using as their town marks a triple castle, three keeps and the Arms of the City of Chester respectively.

By the middle of the 18th century, both Birmingham and Sheffield were fast becoming large manufacturing centres for the trade, and largely through the efforts of Matthew Boulton, the Birmingham industrialist, despite the opposition of the London Goldsmiths' Company, an Act of Parliament set up the Birmingham and Sheffield Assay Offices in 1773, Birmingham taking the anchor as its mark, and Sheffield the crown.

Scotland

In 1457 A.D., James II of Scotland proclaimed a standard of 11 ozs. per lb. troy (i.e. 12 ozs.) for wrought silver. At the same time, the practice of striking a Deacon's (or Warden's) mark alongside that of the maker was instituted. In Edinburgh, the town mark, a triple-towered castle, was used from 1485 onwards, but it was 1681 before a date letter system was adopted. Then, too, an Assay Master's mark was substituted for that of the Deacon, until 1759, when it was replaced by the thistle standard mark.

Scotland was not subject to the Britannia Standard, but in 1720, when sterling was restored in England, the standard of silver was raised in Scotland to conform to the English sterling, 11 ozs. 2 dwts. pure per lb. troy, and the 6d. an ounce duty was also imposed.

In 1586, the Edinburgh Goldsmiths had been granted jurisdiction over the craft throughout Scotland, and that was reaffirmed in 1686, at which time there were goldsmiths recorded as working in Glasgow, Aberdeen, Perth, Inverness, Ayr, Banff and Montrose.

Considerable research has been done in recent years on the Scottish craftsmen outside Edinburgh. Glasgow had its own Incorporation of Hammermen by 1536, and in 1681 they too adopted a date letter system. It fell into disuse in the early 18th century, the letters S (perhaps for Sterling or for Scottish), O and E being much used, together with the town mark, a tree with a bird and bell, and a fish below. Glasgow's industrial growth resulted in the formation, in 1819, of an official Assay Office there, and the lion rampant was chosen as the standard mark. The sovereign's head duty mark was also struck, and in 1914 the thistle standard mark was added. The Glasgow Assay Office, which had been running at a loss for some years, was closed in 1964.

Until the rise of Glasgow, Aberdeen was probably the most important trading centre in Scotland outside Edinburgh, and from about 1600 onwards, various marks were used by the silversmiths, usually in the form of the letters AB, ABD or a contracted symbol, with a single or a three castle mark, very like that used in Newcastle. Aberdeen was actually divided into two burghs, Old Aberdeen, where a pike's head mark is associated with one Colline Allen about 1740/1760, and New Aberdeen, where most of the craftsmen worked.

At Banff, where silver was made from about 1680 to 1830, various versions of the name, from B to BANF were struck. At Dundee a pot-of-lilies appeared on silver from about 1625 to 1810, a device based on the town arms, and at Perth one of several marks used during the long history of silversmithing there was the lion and banner of St. John, though during the 18th century the mark changed to a double-headed eagle, the modern town symbol, which was used until about 1850. Inverness boasted silversmiths for some two centuries, from about 1640 to as late as 1880, a dromedary mark sometimes being used alongside the more usual INS abbreviation. Montrose naturally found itself with a rose mark, seen between about 1650 and 1820, at Arbroath there was a portcullis mark taken from the burgh seal, and at Greenock a "green oak" used from about 1760 to 1840 provided a punning mark much like the T over a tun of Taunton. At Wick and Tain the brief names were usually struck in full, Elgin was contracted to Eln or Elg, and used with a mother and child device said to have been based on the story of a widow who took refuge there in 1745. A tall fort mark has been attributed to Forres, a cross to St. Andrews, and another portcullis mark, with S at the base, to Stirling. Possibly PH stands for Peterhead, where a key mark may also have been used, but much work still remains to be done, not only in identifying town marks but in establishing where some of the itinerant craftsmen worked.

Ireland

Of all the gold and silversmiths in Britain, Ireland's have undoubtedly the longest unbroken history, dating back to the Bronze Age craftsmen. In the Middle Ages, the Dublin gold-smiths were a substantial guild, and in 1555 they were granted a Charter, which was followed by a Royal Charter in 1637. This prescribed the sterling standard, with the harp crowned as the standard mark, superseding a previous, but apparently unenforced, lion, harp and castle. In 1638 a date letter system began, but the series used and even the time each letter was used was somewhat haphazard, and in 1730, when a duty of 6d. an ounce was imposed and the duty paid indicated by a figure of Hibernia, often the date letter was omitted altogether. The Hibernia mark somewhat resembles the Britannia on English silver (as in Scotland, there was no era of Britannia silver in Ireland). Officially, it was struck as a tax "for the encouragement of tillage", but in 1806 Irish silver was struck with the king's head duty mark as well, so that the Hibernia tended to become the Dublin Assay Office mark.

makers mark   Britannia mark   standard mark   date letter

There are very full lists of makers registered with the Dublin Goldsmiths' Company, so that identification of most makers' marks from 1637 onwards is possible. From 1784 onwards, many provincial Irish silversmiths were also registered at

Dublin, and not a few names are recorded in the local records of Cork, Youghal, Galway, and Limerick.

Though no assay offices were authorised outside Dublin (except for one at Waterford to deal with watch cases in 1784 and never apparently put to use) there were guilds in provincial cities. At Cork, goldsmiths were incorporated with other trades in 1656, but most of their records were destroyed in 1891 in a fire at the Courthouse. The names and marks of many Cork goldsmiths are, however, known from the mid-17th century until the beginning of Queen Victoria's reign. A castle, sometimes accompanied by a ship, was used until the early 18th century, when most silversmiths appear to have used their own name punch and the word Sterling or Starling. In Limerick, too, a castle mark was used, from about 1660 to 1710, but after that Sterling in one form or another was usual. Youghal was also identified by a ship mark, a local yawl, and maritime connections were also indicated by the anchor of Galway, used from about 1660 to 1730.

In Ireland, as in England and Scotland, and in the British territories overseas, research goes on, and much still remains to be done in identifying both town marks and maker's marks, and in adding to the small but increasing knowledge of silversmithing in the provinces.

The Use and Abuse of Hall-marks

Obviously hall-marks are a godsend to the silver collector, an invaluable guide to the quality of the metal, the date, the provenance and the maker. But too much reliance on hall-marks, taken at their face value without reference to the piece on which they appear, can be dangerous, and may even lay the collector open to the wiles of the forger.

In reading hall-marks, care should be taken in looking at the shape of the shields, or outlines of the punch; the style of the town mark and the standard mark; the style of the date letter and the actual appearance and crispness of the marks, as well as their position on the piece. Hall-marks are struck with very carefully made dies that leave a sharp impression when they are first punched, and even long years of wear will not usually leave a "soft" appearance which is one of the signs of the faker, who is not usually prepared to spend the time and money making high-grade dies. This is not to say that all "rubbed" marks are suspect, though one should immediately be suspicious of fairly good Britannia marks with very rubbed maker's marks and date letter. Incidentally, very few makers' marks are as crisply struck as the official hall-marks. The placing of the marks is also an important guide: a London-made tankard and cover of 17th century date would have the marks to the right of the handle, near the rim, and another set across the top of the flat cap cover. A mid-18th century one would have the marks on the base. Spoons and forks until 1780 had "bottom marks" near the bowl end, after that they were placed near the end of the stem.

Not all good antique silver bears full hall-marks. Some is completely unmarked, some bears the maker's mark only, struck once or several times. In itself, the maker's mark is not a guarantee of quality, though the assay office at the period could easily have traced the maker from their registers, and many pieces made to special order were not sent for assay due to an interpretation of the law which suggested that only goods "set for sale" were liable for assay. In some instances, the assay offices themselves made errors, omitting, say, the date letter and striking the lion passant twice. But on a fully marked piece, one would expect full marks on the main section, and at least the maker's mark and usually also the lion passant on minor parts, such as the lid of a tankard or coffee pot.

makers mark

standard mark

assay mark

date letter

The status of the hall-mark led to many imitations of it, first among the pewterers and later, in the mid-18th century, by the makers of plated goods. Many marks on Old Sheffield Plate, on close-plated wares and, from about 1860, on electro-plated wares, somewhat resemble silver marks. The imitation marks on Sheffield fused plate in the later 18th century led to restrictions on the type of mark that the platers could register, and most Sheffield Plate marks after 1784 include the maker's full name. Electro-plated wares sometimes also carry hall-mark-like stamps, but often the letters EP, EPNS or EPBM for nickel plated, and Britannia metal wares can be detected, and careful examination of the piece will usually reveal the base metal core.

The reason for hall-marking is to protect the public (in other words, the purchasers) against fraud. However, the long history of hall-marking has resulted in a whole variety of styles of marking, together with some confusing legislation.

The 1973 Hall-marking Act resulted in simplification of the marks, making them easier to recognise and comprehend. In addition, certain other important changes were introduced. One of these was that from 1st January, 1975, platinum had to carry marks. Another change meant that the weight threshold for marking an article is now as follows: silver 7·8g; gold 1g; platinum 0·5g.

British hall-marks consist of a registered sponsor's (maker's) mark, together with the Standard Mark, the Assay Mark and Date Letter (see tables below). Note that Edinburgh uses the Lion Rampant for sterling silver.

THE MARKS ON GOLD

Most of the Statutes regulating hall-marking applied equally to gold, and the marks used were the same as those on silver until 1798, though the standard was changed from time to time. In 1477 it was reduced from 19·2 ct. to 18 ct., but in 1575 it was raised to 22 ct., at which it remained until 1798, being marked with the maker's mark, the lion passant, the assay office mark and the date letter with the sovereign's head duty mark also from 1784. A major change in gold marking in England occurred in 1798, when both 18 ct. and 22 ct. gold were permitted, and were indicated by the relevant figures and by a crown, which replaced the lion passant standard mark. In 1854 three lower standards were introduced, and these were indicated by the carat number plus the value in decimals: 9 with ·375; 12 with ·5 and 15 with ·625. In 1931, 12 ct. and 15 ct. were replaced by 14 ct. (·585) and the crown mark since 1854 has been reserved for the higher 18 ct. and 22 ct. standards. In Sheffield, which obtained a licence to assay goldwares in 1903, the gold mark is a rose (to avoid confusion with the town mark used on silver). In Edinburgh, the Thistle replaces the crown on 18 ct. and 22 ct. gold, while in Glasgow, until its closure in 1964, the Lion Rampant appeared on all permitted standards.

Ireland from 1784 had three standards for gold – 22 ct.

marked with the figures and with the crowned harp and Hibernia; 20 ct. indicated by figures and with a plume of feathers also: and 18 ct. with the figures and a unicorn's head. The crowned harp was omitted from the lower standard goldwares, and on jewellery.

makers mark

assay mark

gold marks

date letter

GOLD MARKS

GOLD STANDARD MARKS

British		Imported
22 carat		*22 carat*
18 carat		*18 carat*
14 carat		*14 carat*
9 carat		*9 carat*

ASSAY OFFICES

British	Imported
London	
Birmingham	
Sheffield	
Edinburgh	

GOLD MARKS

IRISH STANDARD MARKS

22 carat

20 carat

IRISH IMPORTED

22 carat

17

IRISH STANDARD MARKS

18 carat

14 carat

9 carat

IRISH IMPORTED

18 carat

14 carat

9 carat

The Marks on Platinum

Since the introduction of legislation following the 1973 Hall-marking Act all articles containing platinum at 950 parts per 1000 or more must be hall-marked. Alloys below this standard may not be described as platinum.

The first year for marking platinum was 1975, starting with the letter 'A'.

makers mark

platinum mark

assay mark

date letter

PLATINUM MARKS

STANDARD MARKS
British   Imported

ASSAY OFFICES
British   Imported

London

Birmingham

Sheffield

ASSAY OFFICE DATE LETTERS

1544	G	👑	🦁
1545	H	👑	🦁
1546	(letter)		
1547	K		
1548	L		🦁
1549	M		
1550	N		🦁
1551	O O	👑	🦁
1552	P		🦁
1553	Q		
1554	R		
1555	S		
1556	T		
1557	V		🦁

👑

Henry VIII
1547
Edward VI
1553
Mary

G

LONDON

Eliz. I	1558	**a**	1564	**g**	1572	**p**	
	1559	**b**	1565	**h**	1573	**q**	
	1560	**c** **c**	1566	**i**	1574	**r**	
	1561	**d**	1567	**k k**	1575	**s**	
	1562	**e**	1568	**l**	1576	**t**	
	1563	**f**	1569	**m**	1577	**u**	
			1570	**n**			
			1571	**o**			

Eliz. I	1578	**A**	1585	**H**	1592	**P**	
	1579	**B**	1586	**I**	1593	**Q**	
	1580	**C**	1587	**K**	1594	**R**	
	1581	**D**	1588	**L**	1595	**S**	
	1582	**E**	1589	**M**	1596	**T**	
	1583	**F**	1590	**N**	1597	**V**	
	1584	**G**	1591	**O**			

Eliz. I 1603 James I	1598	**A**	1605	**h**	1613	**Q**	
	1599	**B**	1606	**I**	1614	**R**	
	1600	**C**	1607	**K**	1615	**S**	
	1601	**D**	1608	**L**	1616	**T**	
	1602	**E**	1609	**M**	1617	**V**	
	1603	**F**	1610	**n**			
	1604	**G**	1611	**O**			
			1612	**P**			

22

		1625	𝕙	1633	𝕢	James I
1618	𝕒	1626	𝕚	1634	𝕣	1625 Charles I
1619	𝕓	1627	𝕜	1635	𝕤	
1620	𝕔	1628	𝕝	1636	𝕥	
1621	𝕕	1629	𝕞	1637	𝕧	
1622	𝕖	1630	𝕟			
1623	𝕗	1631	𝕠			
1624	𝕘	1632	𝕡			𝕒

		1645	𝔅	1652	𝕻	Charles I
1638	𝔞	1646	𝔍	1653	𝖁	1649 Charles II
1639	𝔟			1654	𝖂	
1640	𝔠	1647	𝔅	1655	𝖃	
1641	𝔡	1648	𝔈	1656	𝖄	
1642	𝔢	1649	𝔜	1657	𝖅	
1643	ff	1650	𝔎			
1644	𝔒	1651	𝔖			𝔞

		1665	𝕳	1672	𝕻 𝕻	Charles II
1658	𝕬	1666	𝕴	1673	𝕼	
1659	𝕭	1667	𝕶	1674	𝕽	
1660	𝕮			1675	𝕾	
1661	𝕯	1668	𝕷	1676	𝕿	
1662	𝕰	1669	𝕸	1677	𝖀	
1663	𝕱	1670	𝕹			
1664	𝕲	1671	𝕺			𝕬

LONDON

Charles II	1678	1683		1691	
1685 James II	1679	1684		1692	
1689 Wm. & My.	1680	1685		1693	
1694 William III	1681	1686		1694	
	1682	1687		1695	
		1688		1696	
		1689		1697	
		1690			

	1697	1702		1710	
William III	1698	1703		1711	
1702 Anne	1699	1704		1712	
1714 George I	1700	1705		1713	
	1701	1706		1714	
		1707		1715	
		1708			
		1709			

	1716	1721	
	1717	1722	
George I	1718	1723	
	1719	1724	
	1720	1725	

Though not compulsory after 1720, the Britannia Standard was sometimes used as an alternative standard. The identifying marks are to be found between 1720 and the present time. A piece of Britannia Silver assayed in 1721 would therefore carry the marks:

LONDON

1726	1732	R	Between 1719 and 1729 one should expect to find numerous variations of the Leopard's Head and Lion Passant marks.	George I / 1727 George II
1727 M	1733	S		
1728 N	1734	T		
1729 O	1735	V		L
1730 P				
1731 Q	Between 1716 and 1728 one should expect to find an occasional variation of the shield shape:			

1736 a	1742 g	1750 p	George II
1737 b	1743 h	1751 q	
1738 c	1744 i	1752 r	
1739 d	1745 k	1753 s	
1740 e e	1746 l	1754 t	
1741 f	1747 m	1755 u	a
	1748 n		
	1749 o		

1756 A	1763 H	1771 Q	George II / 1760 George III
1757 B	1764 J	1772 R	
1758 C	1765 K	1773 S	
1759 D	1766 L	1774 T	
1760 E	1767 M	1775 U	
1761 F	1768 N		
1762 G	1769 O		A
	1770 P		

George III	1776	ⓐ	1783	ⓗ	1791	ⓠ

George III

1776	a
1777	b
1778	c
1779	d
1780	e
1781	f
1782	g

1783	h
1784	i
1785	k
1786	l
1787	m
1788	n
1789	o
1790	p

1791	q
1792	r
1793	s
1794	t
1795	u

An alternative shield may be found.

George III

1796	A
1797	B
1798	C
1799	D
1800	E
1801	F
1802	G

1803	H
1804	I
1805	K
1806	L
1807	M
1808	N
1809	O
1810	P

1811	Q
1812	R
1813	S
1814	T
1815	U

An alternative shield may be found.

George III
1820 George IV
1830 William IV

1816	a
1817	b
1818	c
1819	d
1820	e

1821	f
1822	g
1823	h
1824	i
1825	k
1826	l
1827	m

1828	n
1829	o
1830	p
1831	q
1832	r
1833	s
1834	t
1835	u

LONDON

🦁 🦁 😊		1843	ℌ	1851	ℚ	🦁
1836	𝔄	1844	𝔍	1852	ℜ	William IV
1837	𝔅	1845	𝔎	1853	𝔖	1837 Victoria
1838	ℭ 😊	1846	𝔏	1854	𝔗	
1839	𝔇	1847	𝔐	1855	ℌ	
1840	𝔈	1848	𝔑			
1841	𝔉	1849	𝔒	An alternative shield may be found.		
1842	𝔊	1850	𝔓	▢		𝔄

🦁 🦁 😊		1863	𝔥	1871	𝔮	🦁
1856	𝔞	1864	𝔦	1872	𝔯	Victoria
1857	𝔟	1865	𝔨	1873	𝔰	
1858	𝔠	1866	𝔩	1874	𝔱	
1859	𝔡	1867	𝔪	1875	𝔲	
1860	𝔢	1868	𝔫			
1861	𝔣	1869	𝔬	An alternative shield may be found.		
1862	𝔤	1870	𝔭	▢		𝔞

🦁 🦁 😊		1883	ℌ		🦁 🦁	
1876	𝔄	1884	𝔍	1891	ℚ	Victoria
1877	𝔅	1885	𝔎	1892	ℜ	
1878	ℭ	1886	𝔏	1893	𝔖	
1879	𝔇	1887	𝔐	1894	𝔗	
1880	𝔈	1888	𝔑	1895	ℌ	
1881	𝔉	1889	𝔒			
1882	𝔊	1890	𝔓			𝔄

Victoria / 1901 Edw. VII / 1910 George V

		1903	h	1911	q
1896	a	1904	i	1912	r
1897	b	1905	k	1913	s
1898	c	1906	l	1914	t
1899	d	1907	m	1915	u
1900	e	1908	n		
1901	f	1909	o		
1902	g	1910	p		

George V

		1923	h	1931	q
1916	a	1924	i	1932	r
1917	b	1925	k	1933	s
1918	c	1926	l		
1919	d	1927	m	1934	t
1920	e	1928	n	1935	u
1921	f	1929	o		
1922	g	1930	p		

The Britannia Standard Marks for 1927

1936 Edw. VIII / 1936 George VI / 1952 Eliz. II

		1943	H	1951	Q
1936	A	1944	I		
1937	B	1945	K	1952	R
1938	C	1946	L	1953	S
1939	D	1947	M		
1940	E	1948	N	1954	T
1941	F	1949	O	1955	U
1942	G	1950	P		

LONDON

		1963	**h**	1971	**q**	Eliz. II
1956	**a**	1964	**i**	**1972**	**r**	
1957	**b**	1965	**k**	This sequence was discontinued after the 1973 Hall-Marking Act		
1958	**c**	1966	**l**			
1959	**d**	1967	**m**	1973	**s**	
1960	**e**	1968	**n**	1974	**t**	
1961	**f**	1969	**o**			
1962	**g**	1970	**p**			**a**

		1982	**H**	1991	**R**	
1975	**A**	1983	**J**	1992	**S**	
1976	**B**	1984	**K**	1993	**T**	
1977	**C**	1985	**L**	1994	**U**	
1978	**D**	1986	**M**	1995	**V**	
1979	**E**	1987	**N**	1996	**W**	
1980	**F**	1988	**O**	1997	**X**	
1981	**G**	1989	**P**	1998	**Y**	
		1990	**Q**	1999	**Z**	**A**

2000	**a**				
2001	**b**				
2002	**c**				
2003	**d**				
2004	**e**				
					a

Table 1

			Year		Year	
George III	lion	anchor	1781	I	1790	S
	1773	A	1782	K	1791	T
	1774	B	1783	L	1792	U
	1775	C	1784	M (head)	1793	V
	1776	D	1785	N	1794	W
	1777	E	1786	O (head)	1795	X
	1778	F	1787	P	1796	Y
	1779	G	1788	Q	1797	Z
A	1780	H	1789	R		

July '97 to March '8o. The King's Head is duplicated.

Table 2

			Year		Year	
George III 1820 George IV	lion	anchor	head	1806	i	1815	r
	1798	a	1807	j	1816	s
	1799	b	1808	k	1817	t
	1800	c	1809	l (head)	1818	u
	1801	d	1810	m	1819	v
	1802	e	1811	n	1820	w
	1803	f	1812	o	1821	x
	1804	g	1813	p	1822	y
a	1805	h	1814	q	1823	z

Table 3

			Year		Year	
George IV 1830 William IV 1837 Victoria	lion	anchor	head	1832	J	1841	S
	1824	A	1833	K	1842	T
	1825	B	1834	L (head)	1843	U
	1826	C	1835	M	1844	V
	1827	D	1836	N	1845	W
	1828	E	1837	O	1846	X
	1829	F	1838	P (head)	1847	Y
	1830	G	1839	Q	1848	Z
A	1831	H (head)	1840	R		

🦁 ⚓ 👤		🦁 ⚓ 👤		⚓
	1858 Ⓙ			Victoria
1849 Ⓐ	1859 Ⓚ	1867 Ⓢ		
1850 Ⓑ	1860 Ⓛ	1868 Ⓣ		
1851 Ⓒ	1861 Ⓜ	1869 Ⓤ		
1852 Ⓓ	1862 Ⓝ	1870 Ⓥ		
1853 Ⓔ	1863 Ⓞ	1871 Ⓦ		
1854 Ⓕ	1864 Ⓟ	1872 Ⓧ		
1855 Ⓖ	1865 Ⓠ	1873 Ⓨ		
1856 Ⓗ	1866 Ⓡ	1874 Ⓩ		
1857 Ⓘ				Ⓐ

🦁 ⚓ 👤		🦁 ⚓ 👤		1891 ⓡ		⚓
						Victoria
1875 ⓐ		1883 ⓘ		1892 ⓢ		
1876 ⓑ		1884 ⓚ		1893 ⓣ		
1877 ⓒ		1885 ⓛ		1894 ⓤ		
1878 ⓓ		1886 ⓜ		1895 ⓥ		
1879 ⓔ		1887 ⓝ		1896 ⓦ		
1880 ⓕ		1888 ⓞ		1897 ⓧ		
1881 ⓖ		1889 ⓟ		1898 ⓨ		
1882 ⓗ		1890 ⓠ		1899 ⓩ		ⓐ

Victoria	1900	a	1908	i	1917	S
1901 Ewd. VII	1901	b	1909	k	1918	t
1910 George V	1902	c	1910	l	1919	u
	1903	d	1911	m	1920	v
	1904	e	1912	n	1921	w
	1905	f	1913	o	1922	x
a	1906	g	1914	p	1923	y
	1907	h	1915	q	1924	z
			1916	r		

George V	1925	A	1933	J	1940	Q
1936 Ewd. VIII	1926	B	1934	K	1941	R
	1927	C	1935	L	1942	S
	1928	D	1936	M	1943	T
	1929	E	1937	N	1944	U
	1930	F	1938	O	1945	V
	1931	G	1939	P	1946	W
A	1932	H			1947	X
					1948	Y
					1949	Z

⚓ 🦁		⚓ 🦁		1960	𝕃
1950	𝔸	1954	𝔼	1961	𝕄
1951	𝔹	1955	𝔽	1962	ℕ
⚓ 🦁 ⬭		1956	𝔾	1963	𝕆
1952	ℂ	1957	ℍ	1964	ℙ
1953	𝔻	1958	𝕁	1965	𝟚
		1959	𝕂		

⚓ George VI
1952 Eliz. II

Ⓐ

⚓ 🦁		1969	𝕌	⚓ 🦁	
1966	ℝ	1970	𝕍	1973	𝕐
1967	𝕊	1971	𝕎	⚓ 🦁	
1968	𝕋	1972	𝕏	1974	ℤ

⚓ Eliz. II

ℝ

⚓ 🦁		1985	𝓛	1996	𝕎
1975	𝒜	1986	𝓜	1997	𝕏
1976	ℬ	1987	𝓝	1998	𝕪
1977	𝒞 👤	1988	𝓞	1999	ℤ ✠
1978	𝒟	1989	𝓟	2000	𝕒 ✠
1979	ℰ	1990	𝓠	2001	𝕓
1980	ℱ	1991	𝓡	2002	𝕔 👤
1981	𝒢	1992	𝓢	2003	𝕕
1982	ℋ	1993	𝓣	2004	𝕖
1983	𝒥	1994	𝓤		
1984	𝒦	1995	𝓥		

⚓

𝒜

𝕒

33

CHESTER

1680		1690		1690 to 1700

Charles II

1685 James II

1689 Wm. & My.

1694 William III

1701	A	1709 I	1718 S
1702	B	1710 K	1719 T
1703	C	1711 L	1720 U
1704	D	1712 M	1721 V
1705	E	1713 N	1722 W
1706	F	1714 O	1723 X
1707	G	1715 P	1724 Y
1708	H	1716 Q	1725 Z
		1717 R	

William III

1702 Anne

1714 George I

1726	A	1734 J	1743 J
1727	B	1735 K	1744 J
1728	C	1736 L	1745 U
1729	D	1737 M	1746 V
1730	E	1738 N	1747 W
1731	F	1739 O	1748 X
1732	G	1740 P	1749 Y
1733	H	1741 Q	1750 Z
		1742 R	

George I

1727 George II

🦁 😺 🛡	1759 i	1768 S	🛡
1751 a	1760 k	1769 T	😺
1752 b	1761 l	1770 U	
1753 c	1762 m	1771 U	George II
1754 d	1763 n	1772 V	1760 George III
1755 e	1764 O	1773 W	
1756 f	1765 P	1774 X	
1757 G	1766 Q	1775 Y	
1758 h	1767 R		a

🦁 😺 🛡	1782 g	1789 O	🛡
1776 a	1783 h	1790 P	😺
1777 b	🦁 😺 ⚜ 🗝	1791 q	
1778 c	1784 i	1792 r	George III
🦁 😺 ⚜	1785 k	1793 S	
1779 d	1786 l 🗝	1794 t	
1780 e	1787 m	1795 u	
1781 f	1788 n	1796 v	a

🦁 😺 ⚜ 🗝	1803 G	1811 P	⚜
1797 A	1804 H	1812 Q	
1798 B	1805 I	1813 R	😺
1799 C	1806 K	1814 S	George III
🦁 😺 ⚜ 🗝	1807 L	1815 T	
1800 D	1808 M	1816 U	
1801 E	1809 N	1817 V	
1802 F	1810 O		A

CHESTER

	1818 Ⓐ	1824 Ⓕ	1833 Ⓟ
	1819 Ⓑ	1825 Ⓖ	1834 Ⓠ
George III	1820 Ⓒ	1826 Ⓗ	1835 Ⓡ
1820 George IV	1821 Ⓓ	1827 Ⓘ	1836 Ⓢ
1830 William IV	1822 Ⓓ	1828 Ⓚ	1837 Ⓣ
1837 Victoria		1829 Ⓛ	1838 Ⓤ
	1823 Ⓔ	1830 Ⓜ	
Ⓐ		1831 Ⓝ	
		1832 Ⓞ	

Victoria	1839 Ⓐ	1847 Ⓙ	1856 Ⓢ
	1840 Ⓑ	1848 Ⓚ	1857 Ⓣ
	1841 Ⓒ	1849 Ⓛ	1858 Ⓤ
	1842 Ⓓ	1850 Ⓜ	1859 Ⓥ
	1843 Ⓔ	1851 Ⓝ	1860 Ⓦ
	1844 Ⓕ	1852 Ⓞ	1861 Ⓧ
	1845 Ⓖ	1853 Ⓟ	1862 Ⓨ
Ⓐ	1846 Ⓗ	1854 Ⓠ	1863 Ⓩ
		1855 Ⓡ	

Victoria	1864 Ⓐ	1871 Ⓗ	1879 Ⓠ
	1865 Ⓑ	1872 Ⓘ	1880 Ⓡ
	1866 Ⓒ	1873 Ⓚ	1881 Ⓢ
	1867 Ⓓ	1874 Ⓛ	1882 Ⓣ
	1868 Ⓔ	1875 Ⓜ	1883 Ⓤ
	1869 Ⓕ	1876 Ⓝ	
Ⓐ	1870 Ⓖ	1877 Ⓞ	
		1878 Ⓟ	

CHESTER

		1897	O	
1884 A	**1890** G	1898	P	Victoria
1885 B	1891 H	1899	Q	
1886 C	1892 I	1900	R	
1887 D	1893 K	An alternative sterling mark used since 1839.		
1888 E	1894 L	An alternative date letter shield used since 1900.		A
1889 F	1895 M			
	1896 N			

		1917	R	
1901 A	**1908** H	1918	S	Ewd. VII
1902 B	1909 J	1919	T	1910 George V
1903 C	1910 K	1920	U	
1904 D	1911 L	1921	V	
1905 E	1912 M	1922	W	
1906 F	1913 N	1923	X	
1907 G	1914 O	1924	Y	A
	1915 P	1925	Z	
	1916 Q			

		1940	P	
1926 a	**1933** h	1941	Q	George V
1927 b	1934 i	1942	R	1936 Ewd. VIII
1928 c	1935 k	1943	S	1936 George VI
1929 d	**1936** l	1944	t	
1930 e	1937 m	1945	u	
1931 ff	1938 n	1946	v	
1932 g	1939 o	1947	w	a

George VI	1948	𝒩	1954	D	1961	L
1952 Eliz. II	1949	Y	1955	E	1962	M
	1950	Z	1956	F		
	1951	A	1957	G	In August of 1962 the Chester Assay Office closed.	
	1952	B	1958	H		
𝒩	1953	C	1959	J		
			1960	K		

DUBLIN

1638	Ⓐ	1645	Ⓗ	1652	Ⓟ	
1639	Ⓑ	1646	Ⓙ	1653	Ⓠ	
1640	Ⓒ	1647	Ⓚ	1654	Ⓡ	Charles I
1641	Ⓓ	1648	Ⓛ			1649 Charles II
1642	Ⓔ	1649	Ⓜ	1655	Ⓢ	
1643	Ⓕ	1650	Ⓝ	1656	Ⓣ	
1644	Ⓖ	1651	Ⓞ	1657	Ⓤ	Ⓐ

1658	ⓐ	1665	ⓗ	1672	ⓟ	
1659	ⓑ	1666	ⓘ	1673	ⓠ	
1660	ⓒ	1667	ⓚ	1674	ⓡ	Charles II
1661	ⓓ	1668	ⓛ	1675	ⓢ	
1662	ⓔ	1669	ⓜ	1676	ⓣ	
1663	ⓕ	1670	ⓝ	1677	ⓤ	
1664	ⓖ	1671	ⓞ			ⓐ

1678	Ⓐ	1688-93	Ⓗ	1704	Ⓡ	
1679	Ⓑ	1694-5	Ⓚ	1706-7	Ⓢ	
1680	Ⓒ	1696-8	Ⓛ	1708-9	Ⓣ	Charles II
1681	Ⓓ	1699	Ⓜ	1710-11	Ⓤ	1685 James II
1682	Ⓔ	1700	Ⓝ	1712-13	Ⓦ	1689 Wm. & My.
1683-4	Ⓕ	1701	Ⓞ	1714	Ⓧ	1694 William III
1685-7	Ⓖ	1702	Ⓟ	1715	Ⓨ	1702 Anne
		1703	Ⓠ	1716	Ⓩ	1714 George I
						Ⓐ

39

DUBLIN

George I 1727 George II			1726	𝕲	1736	𝕹
	1717	𝖆	1727	𝕳	1737	𝕽
	1718	𝕭	1728	𝕵	1738	𝕾
	1719	𝕮	1729	𝕶	1739	𝕿
			1730	𝕷	1740	𝖀 𝖀
	1720	𝕬	1731	𝕺	1741-2	𝖂 𝖂
	1721	𝕭	1732	𝕸	1743-4	𝖃
	1722	𝕮	1733	𝕹	1745	𝖄
	1723	𝕯	1734	𝕺	1746	𝖅
	1724	𝕰	1735	𝕻	An alternative Crowned Harp found between 1739 and 1748.	
𝖆	1725	𝕱				

George II 1760 George III			1757	𝕴	1766	𝕾
	1747	𝕬	1758	𝕶		
			1759	𝕷	1767	𝕿
	1748	𝕭			1768	𝖀
	1749	𝕮	1760	𝕸	1769	𝖂
	1750	𝕯	1761	𝕹	1770	𝖃
	1751	𝕰 𝕰	1762	𝕺	1771	𝖄
	1752	𝕱	1763	𝕻	1772	𝖅
	1753	𝕲	1764	𝕼	An alternative Hibernia found between 1752 and 1754.	
𝕬	1754	𝕳	1765	𝕽		

DUBLIN

		1781	𝕀	1790	𝕊	
1773	𝔸	1782	𝕂	1791	𝕋	
1774	𝔹	1783	𝕃	1792	𝕌	George III
1775	ℂ	1784	𝕄			
		1785	ℕ	1793	𝕎	
1776	𝔻	1786	𝕆	1794	𝕏	
1777	𝔼			1795	𝕐	
1778	𝔽	1787	ℙ	1796	ℤ	
1779	𝔾	1788	ℚ			
1780	ℍ	1789	ℝ			𝔸

		1806	𝕂	1815	𝕋	
1797	𝔸	1807	𝕃	1816	𝕌	
1798	𝔹	1808	𝕄	1817	𝕎	George III
1799	ℂ	1809	ℕ	1818	𝕏	1820 George IV
1800	𝔻			1819	𝕐	
1801	𝔼	1810	𝕆	1820	ℤ	
1802	𝔽	1811	ℙ			
1803	𝔾	1812	ℚ			
1804	ℍ	1813	ℝ			
1805	𝕀	1814	𝕊			𝔸

1821	A			
1822	B			
1823	C			
1824	D			
1825	E e			
1826	F			
1827	G			
1828	H			
1829	I			
1830	K			
1831	L			
1832	M			
1833	N			
1834	O			
1835	P			
1836	Q			
1837	R			
1838	S			
1839	T			
1840	U			
1841	V			
1842	W			
1843	X			
1844	Y			
1845	Z			

1820 George IV
1830 William IV
1837 Victoria

A

DUBLIN

1846	â	1855	k	1864	t	
1847	b	1856	l	1865	u	
1848	c	1857	m	1866	v	Victoria
1849	d	1858	n	1867	w	
1850	e	1859	o	1868	x	
1851	f f	1860	p	1869	y	
1852	g g	1861	q	1870	z	
1853	h h	1862	r			
1854	j	1863	s			â

1871	A	1880	K	1890	U	
1872	B	1881	L	1891	V	
1873	C	1882	M	1892	W	Victoria
1874	D	1883	N	1893	X	
1875	E	1884	O	1894	Y	
1876	F	1885	P	1895	Z	
1877	G	1886	Q			
1878	H	1887	R			
1879	I	1888	S			A
		1889	T			

DUBLIN

			1902	𝔊	1909	𝕺
	1896	𝔸	1903	𝕳	1910	𝕻
	1897	𝔹	1904	𝕴	1911	𝕼
Victoria	1898	ℂ	1905	𝕶	1912	𝕽
1901 Ewd. VII	1899	𝔻	1906	𝕷	1913	𝕾
1910 George V	1900	𝔼	1907	𝕸	1914	𝕿
𝔄	1901	𝔉	1908	𝕹	1915	𝖀

			1925	𝔅	1935	𝕿
	1916	𝔄	1926	𝔩	1936	𝖀
	1917	𝔟	1927	𝔪		
George V	1918	ℭ	1928	𝔫	1937	𝖁
1936 Ewd. VIII	1919	𝔇	1929	𝔒	1938	𝖂
1936 George VI	1920	𝔢	1930	𝔓	1939	𝖃
	1921	𝔉	1931	𝔓	1940	𝖄
	1922	𝔖	1932	𝔔	1941	𝖅
	1923	𝔥	1933	𝔕		
𝔄	1924	𝔦	1934	𝔖		

DUBLIN

	1951 **J**	1960 **S**	
1942 **A**	1952 **K**	1961 **T**	
1943 **B**	1953 **L**	1962 **U**	
1944 **C**	1954 **M**	1963 **V**	George VI
1945 **D**	1955	1964 **W**	1952 Eliz. II
1946 **E**	1956 **N**	1965 **X**	
1947 **F**	1956 **O**	1966	
1948 **G**	1957 **P**	1966 **Y**	
1949 **H**	1958 **Q**	1967 **Z**	
1950 **I**	1959 **R**		**A**

	1980 **O**	1994 **I**	
1968 **a**	1981 **P**	1995 **J**	
1969 **b**	1982 **R**	1996 **K**	
1970 **c**	1983 **S**	1997 **L**	Eliz. II
1971 **d**	1984 **T**	1998 **M**	
1972 **e**	1985 **U**	1999 **N**	
1973 **f**	1986 **A**	2000 **O**	
1974 **g**	1987 **B**	1/01–9/02 **Q**	
1975 **h**	1988 **C**	10/02–12/02 **R**	
1976 **i**	1989 **D**	2003 **S**	
1977 **j**	1990 **E**	2004 **T**	
1978 **m**	1991 **F**		**A**
1979 **n**	1992 **G**		**a**
	1993 **H**		

Edward VI	1552		1611		1643
1553 Mary	1563	IC	1617	I·L	1644
1558 Eliz. I	1570		1617	G	1649	GC
1603 James I	1576		1613-21		1651	i·F
1625 Charles I	1585	M	1616-35	G	1660	YB
1649 Charles II	1590		1633		1665	I·S
	1591		1637		1669	
	1591-4	VC	1640		1663-81	E
	1596		1642	IF	1675	
	1609					

1685 James II		B	1689	i		P
1689 Wm. & My.	1681	a	1690	k	1698	S
1694 William III		B	1691	l	1699	t
1702 Anne	1682	b	1692	m	1700	v
	1683	c	1693	n	1701	w
	1684	d	1694	o		
	1685	e	1695	p	1702	x
	1686	f	1696	p	1703	y
	1687	g	1696	q	1704	z
	1688	h	1697	r		

🏰	🌷	1713	I	1721	R	🏰	Anne
1705	A	🏰	EP	1722	S		1714 George I
1706	B	1714	K	1723	T		1727 George II
🏰	EP	1715	L	1724	U		
1707	C	1716	M	1725	V		
1708	D	1717	N	1726	W		
1709	E	🏰	EP	1727	X		
1710	F	1718	O	1728	Y		
1711	G	1719	P	1729	Z		
🏰	EP	🏰	EP				A
1712	H	1720	q				

🏰	AU	1739	K	1746	R	🏰	George II
1730	A	🏰	GED	🏰	HG		
1731	B	1740	L	1747	S		
1732	C	1741	M	1748	T		
1733	D	🏰	EL	1749	U		
1734	E	1742	N	1750	U		
1735	F	1743	O	1751	W		
1736	G	🏰	HG	1752	X		
1737	H	1744	P	1753	Y		
1738	J	1745	Q	1754	Z		A

George II / 1760 George III	(castle) HG	(castle) (thistle)	1771	R
	1755	🅰	1763	J J	1772	S
	1756	B	1764	k	1773	T
	1757	C	1765	L	1774	U
	1758	D	1766	M	1775	V
	(castle) (thistle)	1767	N	1776	X
	1759	E	1768	O	1777	Y
	1760	F	1769	P	1778	Z
	1761	G	1770	Q	1779	U
🅰	1762	H	(castle) (thistle) Alternative town marks sometimes found around 1771.		

George III	(castle) (thistle)	1789	J J	1798	S
	1780	A	1790	K	(castle) (thistle)
	1781	B	1791	L	1799	T (thistle)
	1782	C	1792	M	1800	U
	1783	D	1793	N N	1801	V
	1784	E (head)	1794	O O	(castle) (thistle)
	1785	F	1795	P	1802	W (head)
	1786	G (head)	1796	Q	1803	X
	1787	G	(castle) (thistle)	1804	Y
A	1788	H	1797 R R (head)	1805	Z

EDINBURGH

🏰	🛡️	1814	i	🏰	🛡️		🏰 George III
1806	a 👤	1815	j	1824	s 👤		1820 George IV
1807	b	1816	k	1825	t		1830 William IV
1808	c	1817	l	🏰	🛡️		
🏰	🛡️	1818	m	1826	u 👤		
1809	d 👤	1819	n	1827	v		
1810	e	🏰	🛡️	1828	w		
1811	f	1820	o 👤	1829	x		
1812	g	1821	p	1830	y		
🏰	🛡️	1822	q	1831	z		
1813	h 👤	1823	r				a

🏰	🛡️	1841	K 👤	1851	U		🏰 William IV
1832	A 👤	1842	L	1852	V		1837 Victoria
1833	B	1843	M	1853	W		
1834	C	1844	N	1854	X		
1835	D	1845	O	1855	Y		
1836	E	1846	P	1856	Z		
1837	F	1847	Q				
1838	G	1848	R				
1839	H	1849	S				
1840	J	1850	T				A

49

Victoria			1865	Ⓘ	1874	Ⓢ
1857	Ⓐ	1866	Ⓚ		
1858	Ⓑ	1867	Ⓛ	1875	Ⓣ
1859	Ⓒ	1868	Ⓜ	1876	Ⓤ
1860	Ⓓ	1869	Ⓝ	1877	Ⓥ
1861	Ⓔ	1870	Ⓞ	1878	Ⓦ
1862	Ⓕ	1871	Ⓟ	1879	Ⓧ
1863	Ⓖ	1872	Ⓠ	1880	Ⓨ
1864	Ⓗ	1873	Ⓡ	1881	Ⓩ

Ⓐ

Victoria 1901 Ewd. VII					
1882	ⓐ	1890	ⓘ	1898	ⓡ
1883	ⓑ	1891	ⓚ	1899	ⓢ
1884	ⓒ	1892	ⓛ	1900	ⓣ
1885	ⓓ	1893	ⓜ	1901	ⓥ
1886	ⓔ	1894	ⓝ	1902	ⓦ
1887	ⓕ	1895	ⓞ	1903	ⓧ
1888	ⓖ	1896	ⓟ	1904	ⓤ
1889	ⓗ	1897	ⓠ	1905	ⓩ

ⓐ

EDINBURGH

🏰	🌱	1914	𝕀	🏰	🌱	👑🏰	
1906	Ⓐ	1915	𝕂	1923	𝕊	Ewd. VII	
1907	Ⓑ	1916	𝕃	1924	𝕋	1910 George V	
1908	Ⓒ	1917	𝕄	1925	𝕌		
1909	Ⓓ	1918	ℕ	1926	𝕍		
1910	Ⓔ	1919	𝕆	1927	𝕎		
1911	Ⓕ	1920	ℙ	1928	𝕏		
1912	Ⓖ	1921	ℚ	1929	𝕐		
1913	Ⓗ	1922	ℝ	1930	ℤ	Ⓐ	

🏰	🌱	🏰	🌱	1948	𝒮	🏰	
1931	𝒜	1939	𝒥	1949	𝒯	Ewd. VIII	
1932	ℬ	1940	𝒦	1950	𝒰	1936 George VI	
🏰 🌱 🦁		1941	ℒ	1951	𝒱	1952 Eliz. II	
1933	𝒞	1942	ℳ	🏰 🌱 🦁			
1934	𝒟	1943	𝒩	1952	𝒲		
1935	ℰ	1944	𝒪	1953	𝒳		
1936	ℱ	1945	𝒫	🏰 🌱			
1937	𝒢	1946	𝒬	1954	𝒴		
1938	ℋ	1947	ℛ	1955	𝒵	𝒜	

			1965	k
Eliz. II	1956	A	1966	L
	1957	B	1967	M
	1958	C	1968	N
	1959	D	1969	O
	1960	E	1970	P
	1961	F	1971	Q
	1962	G	1972	R
	1963	H	1973 31st December } 1974	S
A	1964	I		

			1986	M	1998	y
			1987	N	1999	Z ✠
	1975	A	1988	O	2000	a ✠
	1976	B	1989	P	2001	b
	1977	C	1990	Q	2002	c
	1978	D	1991	R	2003	d
	1979	E	1992	S	2004	e
	1980	F	1993	T		
	1981	G	1994	U		
	1982	H	1995	V		
A	1983	I	1996	W		
a	1984	K	1997	X		
	1985	L				

EXETER

X	IOHS			X
1570				IOHS
				Eliz. I
I	n			1603 James I
1571				1625 Charles I
				1649 Charles II
X		X		1685 James II
1575		1680		1689 Wm. & My.
				1694 William III
X			X	
1580			1698	

1701	A	1709	I	1718	S
1702	B	1710	K	1719	T
1703	C	1711	L	1720	V
1704	D	1712	M	1721	W
1705	E	1713	N	1722	X
1706	F	1714	O	1723	Y
1707	G	1715	P	1724	Z
1708	H	1716	Q		
		1717	R		

Anne

1714 George I

A

Table 1 — George I / George II (1725–1748)

Hallmarks	Year	Letter	Year	Letter	Year	Letter
George I / 1727 George II	1725	a	1733	i	1741	r
	1726	b	1734	k	1742	s
	1727	c	1735	l	1743	t
	1728	d	1736	m	1744	u
	1729	e	1737	n	1745	w
	1730	f	1738	o	1746	x
	1731	g	1739	p	1747	y
	1732	h	1740	q	1748	z

Table 2 — George II / George III (1749–1772)

Hallmarks	Year	Letter	Year	Letter	Year	Letter
George II / 1760 George III	1749	A	1757	I	1765	R
	1750	B	1758	K	1766	S
	1751	C	1759	L	1767	T
	1752	D	1760	M	1768	U
	1753	E	1761	N	1769	W
	1754	F	1762	O	1770	X
	1755	G	1763	P	1771	Y
	1756	H	1764	Q	1772	Z

Table 3 — George III (1773–1796)

Hallmarks	Year	Letter	Year	Letter	Year	Letter
George III	1773	A	1781	I	1789	q
	1774	B	1782	I	1790	r
	1775	C	1783	K	1791	f
	1776	D	1784	L	1792	t
	1777	E	1785	M	1793	u
	1778	F	1786	N	1794	W
	1779	G	1787	O	1795	X
	1780	H	1788	P	1796	y

🏰 🦁 👤	1804 **H**	1811 **P**
1797 **A**	🏰 🦁 👤	1812 **Q**
1798 **B**	1805 **I**	1813 **R**
1799 **C** 👤	1806 **K**	1814 **S**
1800 **D**	1807 **L**	1815 **T**
1801 **E**	1808 **M**	1816 **U**
1802 **F**	1809 **N**	
1803 **G**	1810 **O**	

George III

A

🏰 🦁 👤	1824 **h**	🏰 🦁 👤
1817 **a**	1825 **i**	1831 **p**
1818 **b**	1826 **k**	1832 **q**
1819 **c** 👤	1827 **l**	🏰 🦁 👤
1820 **d**	1828 **m**	1833 **r**
1821 **e**	1829 **n**	1834 **s** 👤
1822 **f**	1830 **o**	1835 **t**
1823 **g**		1836 **u**

George III
1820 George IV
1830 William IV

a

🏰 🦁 👤	🏰 🦁 👤	1850 **O**
1837 **A** 👤	1843 **G**	1851 **P**
1838 **B** 👤	1844 **H**	1852 **Q**
1839 **C**	1845 **J**	1853 **R**
1840 **D**	1846 **K**	1854 **S**
🏰 🦁 👤	1847 **L**	1855 **T**
1841 **E**	1848 **M**	1856 **U**
1842 **F**	1849 **N**	

Victoria

A

Victoria (castle)	(castle) (lion) (head)		
1857	**A**	1864	**H**	1872	**Q**
1858	**B**	1865	**I**	1873	**R**
1859	**C**	1866	**K**	1874	**S**
1860	**D**	1867	**L**	1875	**T**
1861	**E**	1868	**M**	1876	**U**
1862	**F**	1869	**N**		
A 1863	**G**	1870	**O**		
		1871	**P**		

Victoria (castle)	(castle) (lion) (head)		
1877	**A**		
1878	**B**		
1879	**C**		
1880	**D**		
1881	**E**		
A 1882	**F**		

GLASGOW

1681	a
1683	c
1685	e
1689	i
1690	K

1694	o
1696	q
1698	s
1699	t

1700	u
1701	v
1704	y
1705	z
1707	B
1709	D

Charles II
1685
James II
1689
Wm. & My.
1694
William III
1702
Anne

a

1717	
1728	S
1734	S
1743	S
1747	S
1756	S
1757	

1758	S
1763	E
1773	S S
1776	O
1783	S

1785	S
1790	S
1795	S
1800	S
1811	

George I
1727
George II
1760
George III

The makers' marks were stamped in duplicate on either side of the town mark up to 1800.

S

57

GLASGOW

George IV / 1830 William IV / 1837 Victoria	1827 I	1837 S
1819 A	1828 J	1838 T
1820 B	1829 K	1839 U
1821 C	1830 L	1840 V
1822 D	1831 M	1841 W
1823 E	1832 N	1842 X
1824 F	1833 O	1843 Y
1825 G	1834 P	1844 Z
1826 H	1835 Q	
	1836 R	

Victoria	1853 I	1862 R
1845 A	1854 J	1863 S
1846 B	1855 K	1864 T
1847 C	1856 L	1865 U
1848 D	1857 M	1866 V
1849 E	1858 N	1867 W
1850 F	1859 O	1868 X
1851 G	1860 P	1869 Y
1852 H	1861 Q	1870 Z

58

GLASGOW

🛡️ 🦁 👤	1879	I	1888	R	🛡️ Victoria
1871 A	1880 J	1889 S	
1872 B	1881 K	1890 T	
1873 C	1882 L	1891 U	
1874 D	1883 M	1892 V	
1875 E	1884 N	1893 W	
1876 F	1885 O	1894 X	
1877 G	1886 P	1895 Y	
1878 H	1887 Q	1896 Z	A

🛡️ 🦁	1906 𝒥	🛡️ 🦁 🌸	🛡️ Victoria
1897 𝒜	1907 𝒦	1914 ℛ	1901 Ewd. VII
1898 ℬ	1908 ℒ	1915 𝒮	1910 George V
1899 𝒞		1916 𝒯	
1900 𝒟	1909 ℳ	1917 𝒰	
1901 ℰ	1910 𝒩	1918 𝒱	
1902 ℱ	1911 𝒪	1919 𝒲	
1093 𝒢		1920 𝒳	
1904 ℋ	1912 𝒫	1921 𝒴	
1905 ℐ	1913 𝒬	1922 𝒵	A

59

GLASGOW

George V / 1936 Ewd. VIII / 1936 George VI	1923 **a**	1932 **j**
	1924 **b**	1933 **k**
	1925 **c**	1934 **l**
	1926 **d**	1935 **m**
	1927 **e**	1936 **n**
	1928 **f**	1937 **o**
	1929 **g**	1938 **p**
	1930 **h**	1939 **q**
	1931 **i**	1940 **r**

1941 **s**	
1942 **t**	
1943 **u**	
1944 **v**	
1945 **w**	
1946 **x**	
1947 **y**	
1948 **z**	

George VI / 1952 Eliz. II	1949 **A**	1956 **H**
	1950 **B**	1957 **J**
	1951 **C**	1958 **L**
	1952 **D**	1959 **M**
	1953 **e**	1960 **N**
	1954 **F**	1961 **O**
	1955 **3**	1962 **p**
		1963 **R**

In March 1964 the Glasgow Assay Office closed.

NEWCASTLE

C.1658 to C.1670	C.1685 to C.1694	C.1700	Charles II 1685 James II 1689 Wm. & My. 1694 William III
C.1672 to C.1684	C.1696		

1702 A	1709	1716	1702 Anne 1714 George I
1703 B	1710	1717 P	
1704 C	1711	1718 D	
1705 D	1712 H	1719 D	
1706 E	1713	1720 E	
1707 F	1714 D		
1708 G	1715		A

1721 a	1728 H	1735 P	George I 1727 George II
1722 B	1729 J	1736 Q	
1723 C	1730 K	1737 R	
1724 D	1731 L	1738 S	
1725 E	1732 M	1739 T	
1726 F	1733 N		
1727 G	1734 O	Between 1721 and 1728, the shapes of date shields and lion passant marks often varied. The lion sometimes faces to the left.	a

61

George II	1740 A	1747 H	1755 Q
	1741 B	1748 I	1756 R
	1742 C	1749 K	1757 S
	1743 D	1750 L	1758
	1744 E	1751 M	
	1745 F	1752 N	
	1746 G	1753 O	
		1754 P	

George II 1760 George III	1759 A	1775 I	1782 Q
	1760 68 B	1776 K	1783 R
	1769 C	1777 L	1784 S
	1770 D	1778 M	1785 T
	1771 E		1786 U
	1772 F	1779 N	1787 W
	1773 G	1780 O	1788 X
	1774 H	1781 P	1789 Y
			1790 Z

George III	1791 A	1799 I	1806 Q
	1792 B	1800 K	1807 R
	1793 C	1801 L	1808 S
	1794 D	1802 M	1809 T
	1795 E	1803 N	1810 U
	1796 F	1804 O	1811 W
	1797 G	1805 P	1812 X
	1798 H		1813 Y
			1814 Z

NEWCASTLE

1815 A	1823 I	1831 R	
1816 B	1824 K	1832 S	
1817 C	1825 L	1833 T	
1818 D	1826 M	1834 U	George III
1819 E	1827 N	1835 W	1820 George IV
1820 F	1828 O	1836 X	1830 William IV
1821 G	1829 P	1837 Y	1837 Victoria
1822 H	1830 Q	1838 Z	A

1839 A	1846 H	1855 Q	
1840 B	1847 / 1848 I J	1856 R	
1841 C	1849 K	1857 S	
1842 D	1850 L	1858 T	Victoria
1843 E	1851 M	1859 U	
1844 F	1852 N	1860 W	
1845 G	1853 O	1861 X	
	1854 P	1862 Y	
		1863 Z	A

1864 a	1871 h	1879 q	
1865 b	1872 i	1880 r	
1866 c	1873 k	1881 s	
1867 d	1874 l	1882 t	Victoria
1868 e	1875 m	1883 u	
1869 f	1876 n		
1870 g	1877 o		
	1878 p		a

Eliz. I		1565	A	1569	E	1590	
1603 James I		1566	B			1595	
		1567	C	1570	F	1600	
				1571	G		
				1573	I	1610	
				1574	K		
A		1568	D	1579	P	1620	

James I	With variations		1630	G	1637	O
1625 Charles I	1624	A	1631	H	1638	P
	1625	B	1632	I	1639	Q
	1626	C	1633	K	1640	R
	1627	D	1634	L	1641	S
	1628	E	1635	M	1642	T
A	1629	F	1636	N	1643	V

C.1645

C.1660

C.1675

Charles I

1649
Charles II

1685
James II

C.1650

C.1665

C.1680

C.1655

C.1670

C.1685

1688

1689

1701

James II

1689
Wm. & My.

1694
William III

1691

1696

1697

SHEFFIELD

👑 George III	🦁	👑	1782	👑		1791	👑
1773	🄲		1783	🄱		1792	🅄
1774	🄵		1784	🄹 ⬛	👑	1793	🄾
1775	🄽		1785	🄿		1794	🄼
1776	🅁		🦁 👑 👤			1795	🅀
👑			1786	🄺		1796	🅉
1777	🄱		1787	🄲		1797	🅇 👤
1778	🅂		1788	🅄		1798	🅅 👤
1779	🄰		1789	🅆		July '79 to March '80. The King's Head is duplicated.	
1780	🄲		1790	🄻			
🄲							
1781	🄳						

👑 George III 1820 George IV	🦁	👑 👤	1807	🅂		1816	🅃
1799	🄴		1808	🄿		1817	🅇
1800	🄽		1809	🄺		1818	🄸
1801	🄷		1810	🄻		1819	🅅
1802	🄼		1811	🄲		1820	🅀
1803	🄵		1812	🄳		1821	🅈
1804	🄶		1813	🅁		🦁 👤 👑	
1805	🄱		1814	🅆		1822	🅉
👑	1806	🄰	1815	🄾		1823	🅄

🦁 👤 👑	1830	g	1837	r	👑 George IV
1824 a	1831 h	1838 S	1830 William IV
1825 b	1832 k	1839 t	1837 Victoria
1826 C	1833 l			
1827 d	👑 🦁	1840 u	
👑 🦁	1834 m	1841 v	🅰
1828 e	1835 p	1842 X	
1829 f	1836 q	1843 Z	a

👑 🦁	1851 H	"	1860 S	👑
1844 A	1852 I	"	1861 T	Victoria
1845 B	1853 K	"	👑 🦁	A
1846 C	1854 L		1862 U	
1847 D	1855 M		1863 V	
1848 E ●	1856 N		1864 W	
1849 F "	1857 O		1865 X	
1850 G "	1858 P		1866 Y	
	1859 R		1867 Z	A

SHEFFIELD

Victoria

	Crown + symbols
A	

Year	Mark
1868	A
1869	B
1870	C
1871	D
1872	E
1873	F
1874	G
1875	H
1876	J
1877	K
1878	L
1879	M
1880	N
1881	O
1882	P
1883	Q
1884	R
1885	S
1886	T
1887	U
1888	V
1889	W
1890	X
1891	Y
1892	Z

Victoria / 1901 Edw. VII / 1910 George V

	Mark
a	

Year	Mark
1893	a
1894	b
1895	c
1896	d
1897	e
1898	f
1899	g
1900	h
1901	i
1902	k
1903	l
1904	m
1905	n
1906	o
1907	p
1908	q
1909	r
1910	s
1911	t
1912	u
1913	v
1914	w
1915	x
1916	y
1917	z

SHEFFIELD

1918	a	1926	j
1919	b	1927	k
1920	c	1928	l
1921	d	1929	m
1922	e	1930	n
1923	f	1931	o
1924	g	1932	p
1925	h	1933	q

1934	r
1935	s
1936	t
1937	u
1938	v
1939	w
1940	x
1941	y
1942	z

George V
1936 Ewd. VIII
1936 George VI

a

1943	A	1953	L
1944	B	1954	M
1945	C	1955	N
1946	D	1956	O
1947	E	1957	P
1948	F	1958	Q
1949	G	1959	R
1950	H	1960	S
1951	I	1961	T
1952	K	1962	U
		1963	V

1964	W
1965	X
1966	Y
1967	Z

1936 George VI
1952 Eliz. II

A

		1974	G
1968	A		
1969	B		
1970	C		
1971	D		
1972	E		
A / 1973	F		

		1983	J	1992	S
1975	A	1984	K	1993	T
1976	B	1985	L	1994	U
1977	C	1986	M	1995	V
1978	D	1987	N	1996	W
1979	E	1988	O	1997	X
1980	F	1989	P	1998	Y
1981	G	1990	Q	1999	Z
A / 1982	H	1991	R		

	2000	a		
	2001	b		
	2002	c		
	2003	d		
a	2004	e		

YORK

During this period several variations of this town mark may be found.

1562	D	1568	K	1575	R	Eliz. I
1564	F	1569	L	1576	S	
1565	G	1570	M	1577	T	
1566	H	1572	O	1582	Z	
		1573	P			
		1574	Q			**D**

During this period several variations of this town mark may be found.

1583	a	1592	k	1596	o	Eliz. I 1603 James I
1584	b	1593	l	1597	p	
1587	e	1594	m	1598	q	
1590	h	1595	n	1599	r	
				1601	t	
				1604	x	**a**

1607	a	1615	J	1624	S	James I 1625 Charles I
1608	B	1616	k	1625	T	
1609	C	1617	L	1626	U	
1610	D	1618	M	1627	W	
1611	E	1619	N	1628	X	
1612	F	1620	O	1629	Y	
1613	G	1621	P	1630	Z	
1614	H	1622	Q			**a**
		1623	R			

71

Charles I 1649 Charles II	1631	a	1638	h	1650	t
	1632	b	1639	i	1651	u
	1633	c	1641	k	1652	v
	1634	d	1642	l	1653	w
	1635	e	1643	m	1654	x
	1636	f	1645	o	1655	y
	1637	g	1649	ſ	1656	z

Charles II			1664	H	1673	R
			1665	J	1674	S
	1657	A	1666	K	1675	T
	1658	B	1667	L	1677	V
	1659	C	1668	M	1678	W
	1660	D	1669	N	1679	X
	1661	E	1670	O	1680	Y
	1662	F	1671	P	1681	Z
	1663	G	1672	Q		

Charles II 1685 James II 1689 Wm. & My. 1694 William III			1689	H		
	1682	A	1690	J	1696	P
	1683	B	1691	k	1697	Q
	1684	C	1692	L	1698	R
	1685	d	1693	M	1699	S
	1686	e	1694	N		
	1687	f	1695	O		
	1688	G				

YORK

1700	1711	1782 G
1700 A	1713	1783 H
1701 B	No records for the period 1714 to 1778.	1784 J
1702 C	1778 C	1785 K
1703 D	1779 D	1786 L
1705 F	1780 E	William III
1706 G	1781 F	1702 Anne
1708		1714 George I
		1727 George II
		1760 George III

1787 A	1795 i	1803 R
1788 B	1796 k	1804 S
1789 C	1797 L	1805 T
1790 d	1798 M	1806 U
1791 e	1799 N	1807 V
1792 f	1800 O	1808 W
1793 g	1801 P	1809 X
1794 h	1802 Q	1810 Y
	1803 and 1806 sometimes faced right.	1811 Z
		George III

1812 a	1820 i	1829 s
1813 b	1821 k	1830 t
1814 c	1822 l	1831 u
1815 d	1823 m	1832 v
1816 e	1824 n	1833 w
1817 f	1825 o	1834 x
1818 g	1826 p	1835 y
1819 h	1827 q	1836 z
	1828 r	George III
		1820 George IV
		1830 William IV

73

YORK

		1844 H	1852 Q
Victoria	1837 A	1845 I	1853 R
	1838 B	1846 K	1854 S
	1839 C	1847 L	1855 T
	1840 D	1848 M	1856 V
	1841 E	1849 N	
	1842 F	1850 O	
A	1843 G	1851 P	

Maker	Location	Date	Mark
William Abdy	London	1784	**WA**
Robt Abercromby	London	1739	**R·A**
,,	,,	1740	**Ab**
Stephen Adams	London	1813	**SA**
Charles Aldridge & Henry Green	London	1775	**C·^HA_G**
Collinc Allen	Aberdeen	1748	**CA**
,,	,,	1748	**CA**
George Angel	London	1850	**GA**
,,	,,	1861	**GA**
,,	,,	1875	**GA**
John Angel & George Angel	London	1840	**J·A &G·A**
Joseph Angel & John Angel	London	1831	**J·A I·A**
Joseph Angel	London	1811	**J·A**
Joseph Angel	London	1849	**J·A**
Peter Archambo	London	1720	**AR**
,,	,,	1722	**PA**
,,	,,	1739	**P·A**
Peter Archambo & Peter Meure	London	1749	**P·A M**
Thomas Bamford	London	1719	**Ba**
,,	,,	1720	**TB**
,,	,,	1739	**TB**
Joseph Barbitt	London	1703	**BA**
,,	,,	1717	**I·B**
,,	,,	1739	**JB**
Edward, John & William Barnard	London	1846	**E·B J&W**

John Barnard London 1702		Peter, Ann & William Bateman London 1800	
,, ,, 1720			
,, ,, 1720		,, ,, 1800	
James Le Bas Dublin 1810		Peter & Jonathan Bateman London 1790	
,, ,, 1819		,, ,, 1790	
John Backe London 1700		Peter & William Bateman London 1805	
,, ,, 1720		,, ,, 1805	
Harry Beathume Edinburgh 1704		William Bateman London 1815	
Hester Bateman London 1761		Joseph Bird London 1697	
,, ,, 1774		,, ,, 1697	
,, ,, 1776		,, ,, 1724	
,, ,, 1778		William Bond Dublin 1792	
,, ,, 1789			

Maker			Mark
George Boothby London		1720	
,,	,,	1720	
,,	,,	1739	
James Borthwick Edinburgh		1681	
Mathew Boulton Birmingham		1790	
Mathew Boulton & John Fothergill Birmingham		1773	
Thomas Bolton Dublin		1701	
,,	,,	1701	
,,	,,	1706	
Thos Bradbury and Sons Sheffield		1832	
,,	,,	1867	
,,	,,	1878	
,,	,,	1885	
Thos Bradbury and Sons Sheffield		1889	
,,	,,	1892	
Jonathan Bradley London		1697	
Robert Breading Dublin		1800	
,,	,,	1800	
John Bridge London		1823	
,,	,,	1823	
,,	,,	1823	
Walter Brind London		1748	
,,	,,	1751	
,,	,,	1751	
,,	,,	1781	
Robert Brook Glasgow		1673	

Alexander Brown Dublin 1735		John Chartier London 1698	
George Brydon London 1720		,, ,, 1723	
,, ,, 1720		,, ,, 1723	
William Burwash London 1802		Henry Chawner London 1786	
,, ,, 1803		,, ,, 1787	
,, ,, 1813		William Chawner London 1819	
		,, ,, 1820	
William Burwash & Richard Sibley London 1805		,, ,, 1823	
		,, ,, 1833	
John Cafe London 1742		Francis Clarke Birmingham 1836	
,, ,, 1742		Nicholas Clausen London 1709	
William Cafe London 1757		,, ,, 1720	
Robt Calderwood Dublin 1727		Jonah Clifton London 1703	
,, ,, 1760		,, ,, 1720	
William Charnelhouse London 1703		John Clifton London 1708	

MAKERS MARKS

Maker	Mark	Maker	Mark
Cocks & Bettridge Birmingham 1806	C&B	Edward Cornock London 1723	EC
Ebenezer Coker London 1739	EC	Augustin Courtauld London 1729	AC
,, ,, 1745	EC	,, ,, 1739	AC
,, ,, 1751	EC	Samuel Courtauld London 1746	S·C
Lawrence Coles London 1697	CO	,, ,, 1751	SC
John Cooke London 1699		Louisa & Samuel Courtauld London 1777	LC SC
Mathew Cooper London 1702		Henry Cowper London 1782	HC
,, ,, 1705	CO	,, ,, 1787	HC
,, ,, 1720	MC	Paul Crespin London 1720	CR
Robert Cooper London 1697	CO	,, ,, 1720	PC
Thomas Corbet London 1699	CO	,, ,, 1739	PC
,, ,, 1699	CO	,, ,, 1740	CR
Edward Cornock London 1707	CO	,, ,, 1757	PC

79

Joseph Creswick Sheffield 1777	**IC**	W. & P. Cunningham Edinburgh 1790	**WPC**
Thomas and James Creswick Sheffield 1810	**T&JC**		
Thomas, James and Nathaniel Creswick Sheffield 1862	**TJ&NC**	Louis Cuny London 1703	**C·V**
,, ,, 1862	**TJ C&N**	Thomas Daniel London 1774	**TD**
William Cripps London 1743	**W:C**	,, ,, 1775	**TD**
,, ,, 1746	**W·C**	,, ,, 1783	**TD**
,, ,, 1751	**W.C**	William Davie Edinburgh 1740	**WD**
John Crouch London 1808	**J·C**	,, ,, 1740	**WD**
Francis Crump London 1741	**FC**	William Dempster Edinburgh 1742	**W·D**
,, ,, 1745	**FC**	William Denny London c. 1697	**DE**
,, ,, 1750	**FC**	William Denny & John Barro 1697	**E B A**
,, ,, 1756	**F·C**	John Denziloe London 1774	
W. & P. Cunningham Edinburgh c.1780	**W& PC**	Isaac Dighton London 1697	**DI**
,, 1790	**W.C PC**	John Downes London 1697	**Do**

Nicholas Dumee London 1776	**ND**	Charles Eley London 1825	**CE**	
John East London 1697	**EA**	William Eley & George Pierpont London 1777	**WE GP**	
John Eckford London 1698	**EC**	William Eley London 1778	**WE**	
,, ,, 1720	**IE**	,, ,, 1785	**WE**	
,, ,, 1725	**EC**	,, ,, 1790	**WE**	
,, ,, 1725	**IE**	,, ,, 1795	**WE**	
,, ,, 1739	**IE**	,, ,, 1795	**WE**	
John Edwards London 1697	**ID**	,, ,, 1795	**WE**	
John Edwards London 1724	**ED**	,, ,, 1825	**WE**	
,, ,, 1724	**I·E**	,, ,, 1826	**WE**	
John Edwards London 1739	**I·E**	,, ,, 1826	**WE**	
,, ,, 1753	**I·E**	William, Charles & Henry Eley London 1824	**WE CE HE**	
		Elkington, Mason & Co. Sheffield 1859	**E M & Co**	

William Elliott London 1813		William Fawdery London c. 1697		
John Emes London 1798		,, ,, 1720		
,, ,, 1802		,, ,, 1720		
Thomas Evans London 1774		Edward Feline London 1720		
,, ,, 1779		,, ,, 1720		
,, ,, 1782		,, ,, 1739		
John Farnell London 1714		William Fleming London c. 1697		
,, ,, 1720		Fenton Brothers Sheffield 1860		
Thomas Farren London 1707		,, ,, 1875		
,, ,, 1739		,, ,, 1883		
John Fawdery London 1697		,, ,, 1888		
		,, ,, 1891		
,, ,, 1720		,, ,, 1896		

Andrew Fogleburg and Stephen Gilbert London 1780	
,, ,, 1780	
Thos Folkingham London 1706	
,, ,, 1720	
William Fordham London 1706	
,, ,, 1720	
Charles Fox London 1822	
,, ,, 1823	
,, ,, 1823	
,, ,, 1823	
,, ,, 1823	
,, ,, 1838	
George Fox London 1861	
,, ,, 1869	

George Fox London 1891	
Charles Thomas and George Fox London 1841	
James Fraillon London 1710	
,, ,, 1722	
William Frisby and Paul Storre London 1792	
Daniel Garnier London 1697	
Robert Garrard London 1802	
,, ,, 1818	
,, ,, 1822	
,, ,, 1847	
Francis Garthorne London 1697	
George Garthorne London 1697	

MAKERS MARKS

Dougal Ged Edinburgh 1734	
Pierre Gillois London 1754	
,, ,, 1782	
James Glen Glasgow 1743	
Elizabeth Godfrey London 1741	
John Goode London 1701	
Andrew Goodwin Dublin 1736	
,, ,, 1739	
Hugh Gordon Edinburgh 1744	
James Gould London 1722	
,, ,, 1722	
,, ,, 1732	
James Gould London 1739	
,, ,, 1747	
,, ,, 1748	
William Gould London 1732	
,, ,, 1734	
,, ,, 1739	
,, ,, 1748	
,, ,, 1753	
Robert Gray & Son Glasgow 1819	
David Green London 1701	
,, ,, 1720	
Henry Greenway London 1775	
William Gwillim London 1740	

William Gwillim & Peter Castle London 1744		Charles Hatfield London 1727		
		,, ,, 1727		
Hamilton and Inches Edinburgh c. 1880		,, ,, 1739		
John Hamilton Dublin 1717		Hawksworth Eyre & Co. Sheffield 1833		
,, ,, 1720		,, ,, 1867		
Charles Hancock London 1799		,, ,, 1869		
,, ,, 1814		,, ,, 1873		
Charles Frederick Hancock London 1850		,, ,, 1892		
,, ,, 1850		,, ,, 1894		
,, ,, 1870		Robert Hennell London 1773		
,, ,, 1870		,, ,, 1809		
John Hardman & Co. Birmingham 1876		,, ,, 1820		
		,, ,, 1826		
Peter Harrache London 1698		,, ,, 1834 (4th generation)		
,, ,, 1698		Robert & David Hennell London 1795 (3rd generation)		

Robert, David & Samuel Hennell London 1802	John Hodson London 1697
Robert & Samuel Hennell London 1802	William Holmes and Nicholas Dumee London 1773
Samuel Hennell London 1811	William Holmes London 1776
Samuel Hennell and John Terry London 1814	Daniel Holy & Co. Sheffield 1776
Henry Herbert London 1734	,, ,, 1778
,, ,, 1735	Samuel Hood London 1697
,, ,, 1739	,, ,, 1720
,, ,, 1739	Charles Hougham London 1773
,, ,, 1747	,, ,, 1785
,, ,, 1747	,, ,, 1786
Samuel Herbert London 1747	Francis Howden Edinburgh 1781
Samuel Herbert & Co. London 1750	Thomas Issod London 1697

John Jacob London 1734		Frederick Kandler London 1758	
,, ,, 1739		Michael Keating Dublin 1779	
,, ,, 1760		,, ,, 1792	
Joseph Jackson Dublin 1799		,, ,, 1854	
Charles Kandler London 1727		William Keats London c. 1697	
,, ,, 1778		,, ,, 1697	
,, ,, 1778		,, ,, 1697	
Charles Kandler & James Murray London 1727		John Keith Banff 1795	
,, ,, 1727		James Ker Edinburgh 1723	
Charles Frederick Kandler London 1735		David King Dublin 1706	
,, ,, 1735		,, ,, 1710	
Frederick Kandler London 1739		George Lambe London 1713	
		Jonathan Lambe London c. 1697	

Paul de Lamerie London 1712		Lea & Clarke Birmingham 1821	**L&C**
,, ,, 1732		Ledsam, Vale and Wheeler Birmingham 1824	**LV&W**
,, ,, 1739		George Lewis London 1699	
John Lampfert London 1748		Charles Lias London 1837	
,, ,, 1749		John, Henry & Charles Lias London 1830	
Louis Laroche London 1725		John & Henry Lias London 1837	
,, ,, 1739		,, ,, 1839	
Samuel Laundry & Jeffery Griffith London 1731		,, ,, 1843	
Thomas Law Sheffield 1773	**T·LAW**	,, ,, 1845	
,, ,, 1773	**T·L**	Henry John Lias & Henry John Lias London 1850	
John Lawrence & Co. Birmingham 1826	**L&Cº**	,, ,, 1853	
Samuel Lea London 1711		,, ,, 1856	
,, ,, 1721		Isaac Liger London 1704	
		,, ,, 1720	

Mathew Linwood Birmingham 1805	**ML**	William Lukin London 1699	**Lu**
John Loyd Dublin 1771	**JL**	,, ,, 1699	**Lu**
Nathaniel Lock London 1698	**LO**	,, ,, 1725	**WL**
,, ,, 1698	**LO**	Ben. Lumsden Montrose 1788	**BL**
,, ,, 1698	**LO**	Mackay and Chisholm Edinburgh c. 1849	**M&C**
Mathew Lofthouse London 1705	**L**	Mappin Brothers Sheffield 1856	**FR & B**
,, ,, 1721	**ML**	,, ,, 1859	**M B**
Mary Lofthouse London 1731	**M·L**	,, ,, 1867	**MB**
Seth Lofthouse London 1697	**Lo**	,, ,, 1867	**EM JM**
Edward Lothian Edinburgh 1731	**E·L**	,, ,, 1878	**EM JM**
Lothian and Robertson Edinburgh 1746	**L&R** **HG**	,, ,, 1883	**C M**
		,, ,, 1885	**FC CH**
		,, ,, 1889	**F.C C.H**
Robert Lucas London 1726	**R·L**	,, ,, 1889	**WG JLL**
		,, ,, 1893	**WG JLL**
James Luke Glasgow 1692	**IL** **IL**	,, ,, 1894	**M BROS** **Mn BROS**

John Newton Mappin London 1882	JNM	Samuel Margas London 1720		
,, ,, ,, 1883	JNM	Thomas Morse London 1720		
,, ,, ,, 1884	JNM	,, ,, 1720		
,, ,, ,, 1884	J·N·M	Marshall & Son Edinburgh c. 1842	M&S	
,, ,, ,, 1885	JNM	Colin McKenzie Edinburgh 1695	MK	
,, ,, ,, 1886	JNM	Lewis Mettayer London 1700	ME	
John Newton Mappin and George Webb London 1866	JNM G.W	,, ,, 1720	LM	
,, ,, 1880	J·N·M G.W	Nathaniel Mills Birmingham 1826	NM	
,, ,, 1880	J.NM C.W	Richard Mills London 1755	R·M	
Jonathan Madden London 1702	MA	,, ,, 1758	RM	
Mathew Madden London 1697	MA	John Moore Dublin 1729	IM	
Jacob Margas London 1706	MA	,, ,, 1740	IM	
,, · ,, 1720	IM	,, ,, 1745	M	
Samuel Margas London 1714	MA			

MAKERS MARKS

Richard Morton Sheffield 1773	**RM**	Mark Paillett London 1698	**PA**	
,, ,, 1773	**RM**	Simon Pantin London 1701	**PA**	
Robert Naughton Inverness 1815	**RN** **RN**	,, ,, 1717	**PA**	
Anthony Nelme London 1697	**Ne**	,, ,, 1720	**PA**	
,, ,, 1722	**N**	Thomas Parr London 1697	**PA**	
Francis Nelme London 1739	**FN**	Thomas Parr Jnr. London 1717	**PA**	
Samuel Neville Dublin 1808	**SN**	,, ,, 1732	**TP**	
Newton & Son Sheffield 1881	**NC**	,, ,, 1739	**TP**	
Henry Nutting & Robt. Hennel London 1808	**HN RH**	,, ,, 1739	**TP**	
Charles Overing London 1697	**DV**	John Parsons Sheffield 1783	**I P & Co**	
Padley Parkin & Co. Sheffield 1846	**P.P & Co**	Humphrey Payne London 1701	**Pa**	
Padley Stanwell & Co. Sheffield 1857	**P.S & Co**	,, ,, 1701	**Pa**	
		,, ,, c. 1701	**HP**	
		,, ,, 1739	**H·P**	

Edmund Pearce London 1704		Peze Pilleau London 1739	
,, ,, 1720		John Pittar Dublin 1751	
William Peaston London 1745		,, ,, 1778	
William and Robert Peaston London 1796		,, ,, 1813	
Samuel Pemberton Birmingham 1784		William Pitts London 1789	
Edward Penman Edinburgh 1706		Pierre Platel London 1699	
James Penman Edinburgh 1705		Philip Platel London 1737	
Phipps & Edward Robinson London 1783		John Pollock London 1734	
		Thomas Powell London 1756	
		,, ,, 1758	
Mathew Pickering London 1703		Joseph Preedy London 1777	
Peze Pilleau London 1720		,, ,, 1800	
,, ,, 1720		John Pringle Perth 1827	
		,, ,, 1827	

Benjamin Pyne London c. 1710		Patrick Robertson Edinburgh 1751	
,, ,, c. 1720		John (later Lord) Rollo Edinburgh 1731	
Phillip Rainaud London 1707		Phillip Rollos London 1697	
,, ,, 1720		,, ,, 1697	
John Rand London 1703		,, ,, 1705	
Samuel Roberts Sheffield 1773		,, ,, 1720	
Samuel Roberts Jnr. & George Cadman Sheffield 1786		Philip Rundell London 1819	
,, ,, 1786		,, ,, 1819	
Roberts & Belk Sheffield 1864		,, ,, 1822	
,, ,, 1864		Abraham Russell London 1702	
,, ,, 1892		John le Sage London 1722	
,, ,, 1869		,, ,, 1739	
,, ,, 1879		,, ,, 1739	

A. B. Savory London 1826		A·B·S
,, ,, 1826		·A·B·S·
,, ,, 1826		A·B·S
,, ,, 1826		A·B·S
,, ,, 1826		A·B·S
,, ,, 1826		A·B·S
,, ,, 1836		A·B·S
John Schuppe London 1753		JS
John Scofield London 1778		I·S
,, ,, 1787		I·S
Digby Scott and Benjamin Smith London 1802		D·S & B·S
,, ,, 1803		D·S B·S
William Scott Banff 1680		WS
James Seabrook London 1714		SL
,, ,, 1720		I·S

Daniel Shaw London 1748		DS
William Shaw London 1727		WS
,, ,, 1728		SH
,, ,, 1739		WS
,, ,, 1745		W·S
,, ,, 1748		W·S
William Shaw & William Priest London 1749		W W·S P
,, ,, 1750		W·S·P
W. & G. Sissons Sheffield 1858		WS C·S
Gabriel Sleath London 1706		SL
,, ,, 1706		SL
,, ,, 1720		G·S
,, ,, 1739		G·S
Gabriel Sleath & Francis Crump London 1753		F G·S C

Benjamin Smith London 1807		Paul Storr London 1807		
Daniel Smith & Robert Sharp London 1780		,, ,, 1808		
,, ,, 1780		,, ,, 1817		
,, ,, 1780		,, ,, 1834		
Edward Smith Birmingham 1833		John Sutton London 1697		
James Smith London 1718		Thomas Sutton London 1711		
,, ,, 1720		John Swift London 1739		
,, ,, 1744		,, ,, 1739		
Stephen Smith London 1865		,, ,, 1757		
,, ,, 1878		James Sympsone Edinburgh 1687		
,, ,, 1880		,, ,, 1687		
Paul Storr London 1799		Richard Syng London 1697		
		,, ,, 1697		

Benjamin Tait Dublin 1791	**BT**	John Tuite London 1739	
James Tait Edinburgh 1704		William Tuite London 1756	**WT**
Ann Tanqueray London 1713		Joseph Turner Birmingham 1838	**I·T**
David Tanqueray London 1713		George Unite Birmingham c. 1838	**GU**
,, ,, 1720		Archibald Ure Edinburgh 1717	**AU**
Joseph Taylor Birmingham 1812	**IT**		
Samuel Taylor London 1744		Ayme Videau London 1739	
Taylor & Perry Birmingham 1834	**T&P**	Edward Vincent London 1739	
Thomas Tearle London 1739		Edward Wakelin London 1747	
Edward Thomason Birmingham 1817	**ET**	John Wakelin & William Taylor London 1776	
,, ,, 1817	**ET**	,, ,, 1777	
William Townsend Dublin 1734	**T·W**	Joseph Walker Dublin 1701	
,, ,, 1734	**WT**		
,, ,, 1753	**W·T**	Samuel Walker Dublin 1738	**SW**

Thomas Walker Dublin 1723		Fuller White London 1750		
Walker Knowles & Co. Sheffield 1836		,, ,, 1758		
Joseph Ward London 1697		John White London 1719		
Samuel Wastell London 1701		,, ,, 1724		
,, ,, 1701		,, ,, 1730		
Mathew West Dublin 1776		George Wicke London 1721		
Gervais Wheeler Birmingham 1835		,, ,, 1721		
		,, ,, 1735		
Thomas Whipham London 1737		Starling Wilford London 1717		
,, ,, 1739		,, ,, 1720		
Thomas Whipham & Charles Wright London 1757		,, ,, 1729		
Thos. Whipham and Wilm. Williams London 1740		David Willaume London 1718		
		,, ,, 1718		
		,, ,, 1728		
Fuller White London 1744		,, ,, 1728		

David Willaume London 1734		Edward Wood London 1740	
Richard Williams Dublin 1761		Samuel Wood London 1733	
,, ,, 1775		,, ,, 1737	
Wilm. Williamson Dublin 1773		,, ,, 1739	
,, ,, 1747		,, ,, 1754	
Joseph Willmore Birmingham 1806		William Woodard London 1741	
Thomas Willmore Birmingham 1789		John Wren London 1777	
,, ,, 1796		Charles Wright London 1775	
John Winter & Co. Sheffield 1836		,, ,, 1780	
John Wirgman London 1751		James Young London 1775	
Edward Wood London 1722		John Young & Co. Sheffield 1779	
,, ,, 1722		,, ,, 1779	
,, ,, 1735			

SHEFFIELD PLATE MARKS

SHEFFIELD PLATE MARKS

The marks to be found on Sheffield Plate have been treated in two sections. The first section includes all of those marks which contain initials. Where a name is provided in the mark, we have listed it under the initial letter of the SURNAME. Where initials only have been used in the mark and because these do not always relate readily to the maker's actual name, we have entered them under the first intial letter, reading left to right. Where, of the initial letters contained, one of them is obviously dominant, we have listed the mark under the dominating letter.

The second small section on p. 114 includes those marks which are of a pictorial nature. In it are contained those marks that bear neither initials nor names.

Ashforth Ellis & Co.	1770	
A. Hatfield	1808	
J. Allgood	1812	
G. Ashforth & Co.	1784	
Ashley	1816	
Askew	1828	ASKEW MAKER NOTTINGHAM
E. Allport	1812	

A

Boulton & Fothergill	1764	
W. Banister	1808	
G. Beldon	1809	
Beldon, Hoyland & Co.	1785	
H. Best	1814	
Best & Wastidge	1816	

B

B

Mark	Maker	Date
W BINGLEY	W. Bingley	1787
Bishop ❀ Bishop	Thomas Bishop	1830
Bradshaw X Bradshaw X	J. Bradshaw	1822
BRITTAIN WILKIN SON & BROWNHILL ○	Brittain, Wilkinson & Brownhill	1785

C

Mark	Maker	Date
☾ ◁ Gilbert ☙ PS	J. Gilbert	1812
♠ Gilbert ♠ Gilbert	J. Gilbert	1812
Gilbert ♣ ♣	J. Gilbert	1812
Cheston ❀	T. Cheston	1809
CHILD ⬎	T. Child	1812
W COLDWELL ☠	W. Coldswell	1806
COPE ⚷	C. G. Cope	1817
CORN &Cᵒ ⊕	J. Corn and J. Sheppard	1819
CRACK NALL ⬏	J. Cracknall	1814
CRESWICKS ✦	T. & J. Creswick	1811

		C
J. F. Causer 1824	**CAUSER** ♛	

		D
D. Not attributed 1760	𝕯 𝕯 𝕯	
J. Dixon & Sons 1835	**D** ✷ **S**	
J. Dixon & Sons 1835.	**D✷S**	
J. Davis 1816	DAVIS **J**	
Deakin Smith & Co. 1785	DEAKIN SMITH & Cᵒ △	
J. Dixon & Sons 1835	*Dixon* ⊖ **J**	
J. Dixon & Sons 1835	G♔R DIXON'S IMPERIAL	
J. Dixon & Sons 1835		
T. Dixon & Co. 1784	DIXON & Cᵒ ✴	
I. Drabble & Co. 1805	I DRABBLE & Cᵒ	
G. B. Dunn 1810	DUNN 🔔	

E	ELL ER BY �֎	W. Ellerby	1803
	S·EVANS ⊃	S. Evans	1816

F	FOX PROCTOR ♥ PASMORE & Cº ✚	T. Fox & Co.	1784
	FREETH ◠	H. Freeth	1816
	✠ ✦ ☺ ◁ HF	H. Freeth	1816
	FROGGATT COLDWELL & LEAN	Frogatt, Coldwell and Lean	1797

G	GA	R. Gainsford	1808
	GH ⚲ ⚲	G. Harrison	1823
	GH ⚲ F	G. Harrison	1823
	GBBS ⊠ ⊠	G. Gibbs	1808
		G. Gibbs	1808
	GARNETT	W. Garnett	1803
	A GOODMAN & Co	Goodman, Gainsforth and Fairbairn	1800

		G
E. Goodwin 1795	E GOODWIN	
J. Green & Co. 1799	I·GREEN&C°	
J. Green 1807	GREEN	
W. Green & Co. 1784	W GREEN &C°	

		H
D. & G. Holly 1821		
Henry Atkin 1823	H A S	
Henry Hall 1829		
Tudor & Leader 1760	H T & C°	
Tudor & Leader 1760		
W. Hutton 1839	H & S	
W. Hall 1820	HALL	
W. Hall 1820		
Joseph Hancock 1755	IOSᴴ HANCOCK SHEFFIELD.	
M. Hanson 1810	HAN SON	
J. Harrison 1809	HARRI SON	
T. Harwood 1816		

H

Mark	Maker	Date
HILL&C°	D. Hill & Co.	1806
HINKS	J. Hinks	1812
HIPKISS	J. Hipkiss	1808
Hob day ◇ Hob day	J. Hobday	1829
HOLLAND&C°	H. Holland & Co.	1784
DAN° HOLY WILKINSON & C°	Dan Holly, Wilkinson & Co.	1784
DAN HOLY PARKER & C°	Dan Holly, Parker & Co.	1804
HOLY S^ C SHEFFIELD	D. & G. Holly	1821
D·HORTON	D. Horton	1808
HOR TON	J. Horton	1809
How. ard	S. & T. Howard	1809
Hutton 2S	W. Hutton	1807
Hutton 2S Sheffield 2S	W. Hutton	1831
Hutton Hutton	W. Hutton	1837

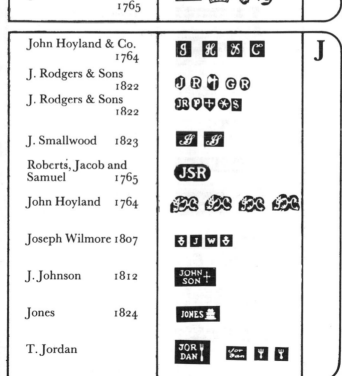

Joseph Hancock 1755	**I·H**	**I**
G. Lees 1811	**I I I**	
I. & I. Waterhouse 1833	*(fleur-de-lis, I & I W & Cᵒ)* *(fleur-de-lis)*	
John Littlewood 1772	**I·L** PLATED	
J. Rowbotham & Co. 1768	**I R**	
John Winter & Co. 1765	**IW** *(crown)* *(device)* *(device)*	

John Hoyland & Co. 1764	**J H H Cᵒ**	**J**
J. Rodgers & Sons 1822	**J R † G R**	
J. Rodgers & Sons 1822	**JR P † ✦ S**	
J. Smallwood 1823	**J J**	
Roberts, Jacob and Samuel 1765	**J·S·R**	
John Hoyland 1764	**JHC JHC JHC JHC**	
Joseph Wilmore 1807	**✦ J W ✦**	
J. Johnson 1812	**JOHN SON †**	
Jones 1824	**JONES ♜**	
T. Jordan	**JOR DAN ♉** *(Jordan)* *(device)* *(device)*	

K	KIRKBY FOR·USE	S. Kirkby	1812

L			
	LAW⊕SON	J. Law & Son	1807
	R.LAW.	R. Law	1807
	𝕋𝕃 THº LAW 𝕋𝕃	Thomas Law	1758
	𝕋𝕃 LAW 𝕋𝕃	Thomas Law	1758
	THO·LAW & Cº	Thomas Law	1758
	A·CLEA ✕	A. C. Lea	1808
	LEES	G. Lees	1811
	LILLY	John Lilly	1815
	JOSʰLILLY	Joseph Lilly	1816
	LIN WOOD	M. Linwood & Sons	1808
	I·LIN WOOD I·LIN WOOD	J. Linwood	1807
	I LIN WOOD I LIN WOOD	J. Linwood	1807
	·LIN WOOD ·LIN WOOD	W. Linwood	1807
	I·LOVE·&·Cº	J. Love & Co. and Love, Silverside, Darby & Co. 1785

		M
Richard Morton 1765		
Richard Morton 1765		
F. Madin & Co. 1788		
Mappin Brothers 1850		
W. Markland 1818		
H. Meredith 1807		
J. Moore 1784		
J. Moore 1784		
F. Moore 1820		
R. Morton & Co. 1785		

		N
Nathaniel Smith 1756		
C. Needham 1821		
W. Newbould & Son 1804		
J. Nicholds 1808		

O		T. Oldham 1860

P		J. Gilbert 1812
		J. Prime 1839
		J. Prime 1839
	JOHN PARSONS & Cº	J. Parsons & Co. 1784
	PEAKE ⋅C	Peak 1807
	PEM BER TON	Pemberton & Mitchell 1817
	PEAR SON	R. Pearson 1811
		J. Prime 1839

R		Robert & Briggs 1860
		Roberts Smith & Co. 1828
	ROBERTS & CADMAN	Roberts Cadman & Co. 1785
	J & S ROBERTS	J. S. Roberts 1786
	ROD GERS	J. Rodgers & Sons 1822

SHEFFIELD PLATE MARKS

J. Rogers	1819	**R**
W. Ryland & Son	1807	

S

J. Smith & Son	1828
J. Prime	1839
S. Colmore	1790
S. & T. Howard	1809
W. Scott	1807
T. Sansom & Sons	1821
R. Silk	1809
J. Shepherd	1817
T. Small	1812
Smith & Co.	1784
Smith, Tate, Nicholson and Hoult	1810
W. Smith	1812
I. Smith	1821

S	JOSEPHUS SMITH	J. Smith 1836
	N·SMITH & C°	N. Smith & Co. 1784
	STANIFORTH PARKIN&C°	Staniforth, Parkinson & Co. 1784
	Stot	B. Stot 1811
	SYKES &C°	Sykes & Co. 1784

T	TB Y S B	T. Butts 1807
	THO MAS	S. Thomas 1818
	THOMASON	E. Thomason & Dowler 1807
		E. Thomason & Dowler 1807
	TONKS	Tonks & Co. 1824
	TONKS □	Samuel Tonks 1807
	TUDOR &C°	Tudor, Leader and Nicholson 1784
	S·TURLEY	S. Turley 1816

SHEFFIELD PLATE MARKS

		T
J. Turton 1820		
J. Turton 1820		
J. Tyndall 1813		

		W
George Waterhouse & Co. 1842		
W. Briggs 1823		
W. Hutton 1849		
W. Jervis 1789		
Waterhouse & Co. 1807		
Watson, Fenton and Bradbury 1795		
Watson, Pass & Co. (Late J. Watson) 1811		
W. Watson 1833	WWATSON MAKER SHEFFIELD	
W. Hipwood 1809		
J. White and White & Allgood 1811		
Joseph Willmore 1807		

SHEFFIELD PLATE MARKS

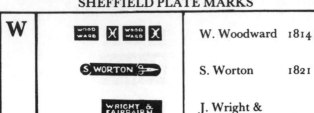

W		
	WOOD WARD ✕ WOOD WARD ✕	W. Woodward 1814
	S WORTON ✂	S. Worton 1821
	WRIGHT & FAIRBAIRN 🎺	J. Wright & G. Fairbairn 1809

Y		
	S C. YOUNGE & C°	S. & C. Young & Co. 1813

PICTORIAL MARKS

✿	✿ ✿	M. Boulton & Co. 1784
	🔗 🔗 🔗	Not attributed 1760
	⛋ ⛋ ⛋	Tudor & Leader 1760
	🜲 🜲 🜲	Fenton Mathews & Co. 1760
	!!!	Not attributed 1760

John Watson & Son 1830		
Padley Parkin & Co. 1849		
Waterhouse Hatfield & Co. 1886		
R. Sutcliffe & Co. 1786		
W. Silkirk 1807		
H. Wilkinson & Co. 1836		
Walker, Knowles & Co. 1840		
Blagden, Hodgson 1821		
Smith, Sissons & Co. 1848		
Roberts, Smith & Co. 1828		

MAKERS MARKS INDEX

NOTES

NOTES

NOTES

NOTES

NOTES

NOTES

NOTES

NOTES

NOTES